EmpowerMoments for the Everyday Woman:
A 31-Day Devotional to Empower Your Womanhood

Tiffany T. Huff

Copyright © 2017 Tiffany T. Huff

All rights reserved.

ISBN-10: 1545324395
ISBN-13: 978-1545324394

Scripture quotations marked (AMP) are taken from the Amplified Bible, copyright © 2015 by The Lockman Foundation. Used by permission of The Lockman Foundation, LaHabra, CA 90631. All rights reserved.

Scripture quotations marked (ESV) are taken from the Holy Bible, English Standard Version, copyright © 2011 by Crossway, a publishing ministry of Good News Publishing. Used by permission of Good News Publishing, 1300 Crescent Street, Wheaton, IL 60187. All rights reserved.

Scripture quotations marked (NASB) New American Standard Bible, copyright © 1960, 1962, 1963, 1968, 1971, 1972, 1973, 1975, 1977, 1995 by The Lockman Foundation. Used by permission. All rights reserved.

Scripture quotations marked (NIV) are taken from the Holy Bible, New International Version, copyright © 1973, 1978, 1984, 2011 by Biblica, Inc. Used by permission. All rights reserved.

Scripture quotations marked (NKJV) are taken from the Holy Bible, New King James Version, copyright © Scripture taken from the New King James 1982 by Thomas Nelson. Used by permission. All rights reserved.

Scripture quotations marked (NLT) are taken from the Holy Bible, New Living Translation, copyright © 1996, 2004, 2015 by Tyndale House Foundation. Used by permission of Tyndale House Publishers Inc., Carol Stream, Illinois 60188. All rights reserved.

DEDICATION

To women around the world who are yearning for growth. May your thirst be quenched.

CONTENTS

Introduction — *Kristen R. Harris* — 2

Superwomen SLAY on Full Tanks
1. Get Your Fill — *Kristen R. Harris* — 4
2. #SLAY — *Chanell Deneá Hill* — 6
3. Is There An 'S' On Your Chest? — *Rodnisha L. Smith* — 8

Crying Is Not Weak; It Makes Me Stronger
4. Liquid Prayers — *Kristen R. Harris* — 11
5. Crying to Your Strength — *Shavon N. Taylor* — 13

I Have Mommy & Daddy Issues
6. A Mother's Love — *Ebony L. Cox* — 16
7. Daddy Issues — *Tiffany T. Huff* — 19

She Has Been Where I'm Standing
8. Peace by Peace — *Jennifer Anthony* — 22
9. Homeless to Happiness — *Gina M. Hall* — 24
10. Exemplify the Love of Christ — *Domini Gamble* — 27
11. Don't Give Up Now — *Keviyona T. Ray* — 30
12. No Pressure, No Diamond — *Keena Miquel Jordan* — 33
13. In An Instance — *Harriet Noel Jones* — 35
14. It's A Journey… — *Sherita Redmond-Yamini* — 37

God's Got Me
15. Be Anxious for Nothing — *Ana M. Jackson* — 40
16. Toy Guns Are Harmless — *Kristen R. Harris* — 43

I LOVE Me
17. Enough Is Enough… — *Marnaé A. Thompson* — 46
18. Self-Love = Self-Confidence — *Tanika McBee* — 49
19. God's Marvelous Works — *LaVonna V. Fields* — 51

The Son Has Set Me Free
20. Defining Moments — *Natalie K. Byrd* — 54
21. He Is Not a Tit for Tat God — *Chanceé Lundy* — 56
22. What Are You Afraid Of? — *LaKeisha Stringfellow* — 58
23. You Have Something to Live For! — *Kristen R. Harris* — 61

I Am Growing Better Daily
24. Pain, Purpose, Power — *Lauran A. Smith* — 65
25. Be GRRREAT! — *Dené M. Brown* — 68
26. Size Doesn't Equate Strength… — *Luronda T. Jennings* — 71
27. Focus On Your Strengths… — *Tchicaya Ellis Robertson* — 74
28. Can You Really Handle It? — *Yerinita T. Curtis-Fuller* — 76
29. Project: Taming My Tongue — *LaVonna V. Fields* — 79

Can't Stop, Won't Stop
30. Don't Stop — *Latasha L. McCrary* — 82
31. Run On In The Rain — *Kristen R. Harris* — 84

Epilogue — *Kristen R. Harris* — 86

Womanhood.

"Anything can happen when womanhood has ceased to be a protected occupation."

~Virginia Woolf

INTRODUCTION

I am so delighted that you have decided to open this book. As you journey through this devotional over the next 31 days, I pray that you have an open mind, a penetrable heart and a receivable spirit. Before this project was even an idea, I was busy praying for you. I prayed that God would heal your spirit. I prayed that He would ignite forgiveness in your heart. I prayed that you would find the motivation you need to stir up the gifts in your belly. I prayed for your shift, your deliverance and that you would find your joyful place. Above all, I prayed that your relationship with the Father would be solidified and glorified.

This book is a compilation of some very powerful women who are sharing their stories of trials and triumphs to answer all of those prayers. Because these beautiful women hail from all walks of life and their experiences run the gamut of reality, I am certain that you will find something that you can relate to very well. These lovely ladies have freely shared some of their deepest secrets and so it goes without saying that this is a judgement-free zone.

In *EmpowerMoments for the Everyday Mom*, I encouraged the women to only read one devotional per day in efforts to truly marinate on the material shared each day. Those moms didn't listen so well and you may not either! That is perfectly okay. If you have skimmed the table of contents and see something that can help you today, then by all means read it today! Or perhaps, your best girlfriend contributed to the book and of course you want to read her EmpowerMoment first. No issue with that either! I just request that at some point you commit to reading the devotionals in chronological order because God organized them in such a way for His divine purposes. Whatever you do, be sure to take a moment daily to EMPOWER yourself!

Lastly, don't be stingy! Share your empowerment with the women around you. After all, we all can use a dose of inspiration each day. If you are so led, please share your journey via text, pictures or video on social media using the hashtag **#EmpowerMoments**. I would love to see you mighty women of God living on purpose!

Alright, enough of the formalities; let's get to the good stuff!

~Kristen R. Harris

Superwomen SLAY on Full Tanks!

"A Superwoman isn't a woman who can do anything, but a woman who avoids doing too much."

~Shirley Conran

1 GET YOUR FILL
Kristen R. Harris

Satisfy us in the morning with your steadfast love, that we may rejoice and be glad all our days. Psalm 90:14 ESV

In the morning, Lord, you hear my voice; in the morning I lay my requests before you and wait expectantly. Psalm 5:3 NIV

During the school year, my weekday morning routine is pretty consistent. Cook breakfast, pack lunches, check backpacks, transport kids to school, and return home to get my work day started. However, sometimes a monkey wrench is tossed into my plans and my morning routine is completely knocked out of kilter. Such was the case one morning as we were on our way to school and I ran out of gas! The fact that I hate pumping gas is no mystery to my close friends. Thus, I often ride until I use the very last drop of fuel in my tank. I'm notorious for the line, *"Oh, I know my car. We can make it a few more miles."* Well that morning my few more miles ran out!

As we waited for assistance on the side of the road, my eldest daughter so innocently inquired, *"The day just started, so why don't we have any gas in our car?"* The most honest and intelligent answer that I could conjure up was simply, *"Because I didn't fill up."* I caught a glance of her reaction in my rear view mirror. Her bewildered expression spoke to me loud and clear. *How can you expect your car to keep running if you are not filling it up regularly?* And that, lovely ladies, is where our EmpowerMoments journey will begin!

As women we wear several different hats — wife, mother, daughter, sister, friend, leader, employee, employer, minister, etc. As soon as we walk out of our homes each day, we have to hit the ground running fulfilling each of those roles. If we are not careful, we will find ourselves running and running and never filling up. That system leaves us depleted, exhausted, and burned out. More important, never replenishing our spiritual tank leaves us vulnerable to the enemy's attacks. As essential as fuel is to making our vehicles operate properly, so is taking time each day to fill our spirits up to effectively be the women that God called us to be.

Spending time studying and meditating on God's word each day reminds you of His promises for your life. It also has the power to energize and uplift when you are feeling discouraged. Communicating with Him each morning allows you to empty your issues at His feet while He fills you up with His love, His grace, His strength and His plan for your day. It's everything you need to get through what lies ahead.

May the God of hope fill you with all joy and peace as you trust in him, so that you may overflow with hope by the power of the Holy Spirit. Romans 15:13 NIV

If you are reading this EmpowerMoment, you have taken the first step to making a commitment to get your fill each day. For the next 30 days, spend some time getting recharged as you read through the daily EmpowerMoments. I have prayed that this is only a starting point for you as you seek to dig deeper into understanding God's will for your life. When you feel empowered, please don't be stingy. Share the empowerment and enlightenment that you receive with another woman you encounter on your day's journey.

Let us pray:

Dear Daddy,
I understand how important it is to spend time with You before I start my day each morning. Every morning I want to seek You for direction for my day. Please fill me up with Your love, wisdom and strength so that I may conquer anything that comes my way. Lord, as I stand at the beginning of a new thirty-one day devotional, please help me to complete my commitment. I am excited about the revelation that You will share with me on this journey. In Jesus' Name, Amen!

Today I EMPOWER you to pull up to the station and get your spiritual fill-up each morning before you step out to meet all that the world will bring you. I EMPOWER you to make a habit of meditating on God's word and spending time in prayer each morning, starting with the next 30 days, as you commit to reading your daily EmpowerMoments. Take a moment daily to EMPOWER yourself!

2 #SLAY
Chanell Deneá Hill

Charm is deceptive, and beauty is fleeting; but a woman who fears the LORD is to be praised. Proverbs 31:30 NIV

Last January I joined a bikini challenge at a premier and popular gym in my neighborhood. The weight loss program was six months and included a team according to body types, meals plans and so much more. The gym focused on sisterhood, accountability and hard work and I was so elated to join. One requirement for the challenge was that participants had to take at least seven 1-hour classes or more per week. At the beginning of the program I was very committed taking as many classes as I could. As the challenge continued, I even found myself, with majority of the other women, working out two times or sometimes three times a day. The gym began to become a top priority in my life and I found myself neglecting many important areas in my life. Sadly, I even started abandoning my personal study, worship time and even church services to either sleep, go to the gym and/or gym team meetings

The weight was coming off and I was looking great. Oh honey, I thought I was slaying the game with my new slim body, shoes, whipped hair and cute outfits. However, as I was abandoning time to build up my spiritual man, I begin to notice bad behaviors occurring, mental warfare and so much more. Due to neglect I willingly left an open door for the devil to come in and wreak havoc in my life. I was so focused on my goal that I forgot about the ULTIMATE goal. I was slaying everything but the devil! Sadly, many of my sisters are doing the same thing. We focus more on our outer beauty, disregarding my inner beauty. Slaying the game but destroying my armor.

Sisters, God has called us to #slay more than a cute body, hair and make-up. He has called us to be mighty women of God in His kingdom, slaying the enemy of darkness around us. Charm is "deceitful" in that it is short-term. Beauty is "vain" in that it is shallow. But a woman who fears the LORD is to be praised; her reverence for God endures forever.

We are assured in God's word that He desires for His daughters to be beautiful. Now, let's be clear. God is not telling us to neglect our temple, or not to look our best. God is the creator of beauty, but He has warned us about building our lives on self-images. He desires His daughters to be of power, authority and substance more than our looks. Sisters, you better *werk*, but don't let it stop just there. Balance your life and make sure the inner woman is taken care of. Luke 10:9 affirms that we have the power to tread over the head of scorpions and the devil. Are we using that power if we are spending hours on end in the gym, make-up chair or hair salon, only concerned with beautifying our outward appearances?

After a mental break down at the gym, I decided to take a step back and get ME back together. As I started to reconnect with God and build back up the full armor of Christ, my mind became clearer and the pressure relieved. Yes, I still workout weekly. However, I no longer abandon my personal time with God. If I sit in the sauna, I'm readying my word. Walking on the treadmill I'm listening to worship music. I also make sure I am in bible study and church service. These are small and simple things to help me stay close to him. I asked God to help me balance slaying the game in taking care of my temple and my inner beauty. He has answered my prayers and guided me along the way. If I start to stray in putting my focus in another area and neglect him, he doesn't hesitate to convict me.

Sisters, let's root our identity in God. Let's #slay by putting God first in all we do. #Slay by walking in who God has created you to be. #Slay by putting your high heels on the neck of the enemy. The devil isn't frightened of a woman whose face is beat or whose feet are laced with red bottoms, but one that walks in the authority and power given to her by Christ.

Dear Daddy,
I thank You for how beautifully You have created me. Please, God, don't allow me to become so caught up in my looks that I neglect my heart. Help me to find balance in my daily life. For I know You don't look at my appearance, but You look at my heart. Let me do a heart check to make sure I align up with You and Your word. God, if I start to spend more time on my appearance or even think too haughtily of myself, humbly remind me that my purpose isn't to #slay for the world but to bring You glory and #slay the enemy daily. Teach me to #slay in prayer, worship and love. In Jesus' Name, Amen!

Ladies, I EMPOWER you to take an inventory of what you spend time doing every day. If you are lacking in personal time, rearrange, delete and create an allotted time for you to spend quality moments with God. Make time with God a priority!

3 IS THERE AN 'S' ON YOUR CHEST?
Rodnisha L. Smith

But when He, the Spirit of Truth (the Truth-giving Spirit) comes, He will guide you into all the Truth (the whole, full Truth). For He will not speak His own message [on His own authority]; but He will tell whatever He hears [from the Father; He will give the message that has been given to Him], and He will announce and declare to you the things that are to come [that will happen in the future]. He will honor and glorify Me, because He will take of (receive, draw upon) what is Mine and will reveal (declare, disclose, transmit) it to you. John 16:13-14 AMP

For many years I have been the "go-to person." People always seem to think that I can solve any situation. Because I have been relied on in this capacity, I started to believe this was true. From this, an agenda or schedule rarely existed and caused a serious overload in my life. However, I would keep going because I knew helping people was the "right thing to do." I was just like the Energizer Bunny or more like Superwoman! I would go and go and go and go, complete with the cape around my neck and 'S' on my chest! I arrived on the scene and you would hear, "Bum, bum, bum, bummmm!" After a while, "bum, bum, bum, bummmm" turned into frustration, the cape was wrinkled, and the 'S' withered. Then I heard His voice, *"Did **I** tell you to do that?"*

Trust in the LORD with all thine heart; and lean not unto thine own understanding. In ALL thy ways acknowledge him, and he shall direct thy paths. Proverbs 3:5-6 KJV

Do you make plans daily without permission or direction from God? Do you find yourself doing things because you think it's the right thing to do? Do you operate with an 'S' on your chest? Great, if you do because you should! However, that 'S' should stand for Spirit! In everything we do, we should be Spirit-led! It is unfortunate that God provides us with spiritual navigation but we don't use it. We prefer to drive in circles as opposed to getting directions from the One who knows the destination! The Holy Spirit knows the plan of the Father and desires to give it to us, but we must be in relationship with Him. God, the Father, tells Jesus His plan then Jesus shares it with the Holy Spirit. It is our job to spend time in the Word and prayer to get revelation of the plan of God. Giving directions isn't the only job of the Holy Spirit; the Holy Spirit has several jobs that are important to us.

And I will ask the Father, and He will give you another Comforter (Counselor, Helper, Intercessor, Advocate, Strengthener, and Standby), that He may remain with you forever. John 14:16 AMP

God loves us so much. It is not His plan that we are overloaded. He has given us a helper and it is our responsibility to seek and receive His help. The counsel from the Counselor will guide you to winning strategies so every area of your life will be super by way of His Spirit. Please embark on a journey of truly allowing God's Spirit to lead you. There are some excellent things that God desires to happen; however, they cannot be fulfilled without intimacy with the Spirit of God and His leading.

Dear Daddy,
I ask for Your forgiveness for endeavoring to live without Your Holy Spirit. Father, I welcome the Holy Spirit to lead and guide me to all truths. I will acknowledge You in all my ways. I give You permission to direct my path and order my steps. I thank You, Lord, for a spirit of conviction if I endeavor to do anything without You! Holy Spirit, take over my will right now. In Jesus' Name, Amen!

Ladies, I EMPOWER you to remove the Superwoman off your chest and replace it with Spirit-led Woman! I EMPOWER you to allow the Spirit of the true and living God to lead you so that you can receive the results God desires for your life! I decree and declare that when you place Spirit-led Woman across your chest and allow God to lead, you will prosper, have peace, and be productive.

Crying Is Not Weak; It Makes Me Stronger.

"We need never be ashamed of our tears."
~Charles Dickens

4 LIQUID PRAYERS
Kristen R. Harris

You keep track of all my sorrows. You have collected all my tears in your bottle. You have recorded each one in your book. Psalm 56:8 NLT

    6:15 am – My alarm goes off and I'm mad that I have to get up to go to a job that I strongly dislike. I'm not being successful in life because I'm not pursuing my purpose and passions! **6:25 am** – I realize that my baby is sick but I can't afford to stay at home and nurse her back to health; I have to go to the job that I strongly dislike. Being a working mom is so hard and at times I feel like I'm a terrible mother. **7:00 am** - I go outside to race my sick daughter to school because I can't stay home with her because I have to go to the job that I strongly dislike and I find a $250.00 ticket on my windshield. *Failure to display a village sticker* –There is no one to blame but me; I'm so irresponsible at times. **7:15 am** – I call my husband to vent about my $250.00 ticket on the car that I'm driving our sick daughter to school in and then heading to the job that I strongly dislike and he irritates me even more. He was really only trying to help but I snapped back because I didn't want to hear what he was saying; I'm such a horrible person right now. **7:30 am** – I'm in the middle of rush hour traffic, my girls are in the backseat singing along to Kirk Franklin's "Give Me" and I just lose it. Right there on Interstate 57, I have an emotional breakdown and start crying a river on my steering wheel. "*Why is there SO much pressure,*" I ask God. I quickly try to compose myself because I don't want my kids to worry but the more I try to suppress the tears, the more they flow. In the midst of my release, God reminded me of one my favorite scriptures: **You keep track of all my sorrows. You have collected all my tears in your bottle. You have recorded each one in your book. Psalm 56:8**

    Wow, God loves me so much that He is literally recording each one of my sorrows. The job, the sick child, the ticket, the husband, the frustrations, everything is being accounted for in His book. That means that He *really* loves me! I remember once trying to stifle tears (as I usually do) after a heart wrenching incident and a wise woman told me not to hold back my tears because they were liquid prayers. That theory has stuck with me because I always feel better after I pray and likewise after I cry. The situation may not change, but God always changes a piece of me in prayer. So there I was watering my black slacks with prayers. My tears were speaking to God because I didn't even know what I needed to say or what I needed Him to do; I just knew that I needed some help! But the Holy Spirit was right there speaking through my tears! **If we don't know how or what** to pray, it doesn't matter. He does our praying in and for us, making prayer out of our wordless sighs, our aching groans. **Romans 8: 26 MSG**

After I was done crying a river, I asked God why on earth would He want to bottle every tear this cry baby releases. His wise response reminded me of why I serve only Him! **"Every time you cry, I make sure I'm there to wipe your tears away so that each one is caught in my hands and can be placed in a bottle. (Isaiah 25:8) As liquid prayers, I store them up and use them to water the very situation that caused them. This bottle of tears about your job will water your future business so that it may grow into a successful venture. This bottle of tears about your ill child will be used to water her healing and distinguish the fire of more serious illnesses that the enemy will try to cripple her with. This bottle of tears for your ticket is to water your responsibility so that you may grow into the Proverbial 31 woman I designed you to be. Your bottle of tears for your husband will be used to water you into a wife whose words are like honey (Psalm 16:24). And then I have this bottle of miscellaneous tears. They are from the times when you were overcome with emotion and didn't know why. I pour these out on the extra stuff every time I just want to show you favor for those who sow in tears will reap with songs of joy! (Psalm 126:5)"** Needless to say, I started crying all over again!

Dear Daddy,
I thank You for giving me an avenue of release and prayer through crying. What the world thinks is a sign of weakness, You are using to strengthen our relationship! I thank You for bottling each of my tears and using them to water the dry places in my life. You are such a compassionate God and I'm grateful that I can come to You in my most vulnerable state. Please continue to keep me close. In Jesus' Name, Amen!

Ladies, today EMPOWER your tears for they are liquid prayers. Sometimes we just need to release everything that's bottled up inside. If you're at work, take a bathroom break and let it out! Crying may be a sign of weakness to the world but God is using your bottled tears to strengthen your life!

5 CRYING TO YOUR STRENGTH
Shavon N. Taylor

In my distress I called to the Lord; I cried to my God for help. From his temple he heard my voice, my cry came before him, into his ears. Psalm 18:6 NIV

My friend Carla, whom I love dearly, is considered to be the "rock" of our sister circle. She is a "tough cookie" and not easily affected by circumstances. Unlike her, I am the sensitive one of our inner circle—and will cry in a heartbeat. We nicknamed Carla, "Rocky," because she is the epitome of having thick skin. In fact, a *strong* woman is often characterized as being a rock or a pillar of strength. Even in my family structure, being strong was so important that in thirty years, I had not seen too many of my aunts, cousins, or even my own mother cry. Like "Rocky," I can remember the women in my family giving me sound advice about not being weak or the shame in crying too much. Most times, in dealing with painful circumstances, Rocky would shrug her shoulders and say to me, "Girl, it is what it is." I marveled at how my friend had so much resilience and tenacity that I would often say to her that I had wished I had a little piece of her inside me. But back to this rock characteristic. Biblically, rocks are symbols of strength and permanence and places where people often took refuge. As Christian women, we know that Jesus Christ is our Rock! Yes, we praise God for being the rock of our salvation, our Chief Cornerstone, the Rock in a weary land and I could spend hours testifying about God, our Rock! God, through His word, reminds us that it is His strength we are to rely on and it is in Him that we take refuge.

As I grew older, I realized that my friend and the strong women in my family, including my mother, had this "rock thing" wrong. In fact, not seeing "Rocky" cry was almost unnatural because I knew she had many troubled days filled with hurts and losses. Perhaps, she had cried plenty of times but thought by suppressing her tears that she was protecting herself or others in some way.

I am certain that my friend is not the only woman who has stifled her tears. I have known many women who may have lost a loved one or may have ended a relationship or dealt with some type of stressful situation only to hear their support system say things like, "Girl, don't cry" or "Stop all that crying" or my personal favorite, "I wouldn't be crying." But why not cry? Crying is therapeutic. Crying releases the pain and most of all, God wants to hear our cries for His strength is made perfect in our weakness. In other words, when we cry out to God we get to witness first hand exactly who He is and what He is made of because that is what a Father does for His daughters.

Honestly, sometimes as women, we work so hard trying to be strong for everyone we encounter. We nurture our spouses, children, family members, and friends until it hurts us. We are quick to wipe our tears in shame so that no one sees us. In **Psalm 18**, we find a great lesson from one of the strongest warriors God ever used—David. And if David can cry out, guess what, so can we! Additionally, in **Psalm 55:22**, David implores us to **cast our cares on the Lord**. Even when such cares make us cry, we are able to give them to the Lord.

The next time you feel like crying, do it! The next time you are sad, hurt, confused and tired, cry unto the Lord. Allow God to see that you need His help and that you rely on His strength. Always remember, He is our Rock and it's never the other way around.

Dear Daddy,
Thank You for being my Rock! Thank You for hearing my cries and my pleas for Your help. You are the only one to wipe my tears and not leave me feeling shameful. Thank You for Your supernatural strength and authority. I will always remember to cast my cares upon You. I love You, I trust You and I need You always. In Jesus' Name, Amen!

Ladies, I EMPOWER you to cry out unto the Lord when you are perplexed, hurt, have feelings of despair and are in need of help. Instead of unleashing your emotional well-being into the world of social media, God is waiting to hear from you! He will hear you just as he heard David. Find a quiet space where you and your Heavenly Father can convene and cry out to Him! Next, arise victoriously because you have left the matter in the Master's hands.

I Have Mommy & Daddy Issues.

"Children begin by loving their parents; as they grow older they judge them; sometimes they forgive them."

~Oscar Wilde

6 A MOTHER'S LOVE
Ebony L. Cox

"Honor your father and mother"—which is the first commandment with a promise... Ephesians 6:2 NIV

It's been almost 5 years since I sat in the hospital and watched my mother slowly deteriorate and pass away. I sat around family and close friends in the days leading up to the inevitable truth of what we all knew would happen. That's when I sat by her bedside, looking at her knowing that any day could be her last and struggling with the fact that I still hadn't found it within myself to forgive her.

Rewind to 2002-- When I was about 14 years old, I moved in with my godmother who stayed a block away from my house. My mother was going through hard times and thought it best to have my siblings and me around family that could take care of and love us until she was well and back on her feet. My siblings moved to Milwaukee with their father's family and since I was already so close to my 8th grade promotion, it made more sense for me to stay in Waukegan, Illinois and finish out the school year. On one hand, I was happy to be with my god sisters and brothers who were all around my age, but on the other I missed my siblings like crazy. I had so many questions that ran through my mind each night. *"When would she come back for us? Would she ever be okay? Would my siblings forget me?"* Thoughts upon thoughts consumed me and ate at me daily.

The positive side was that my godmother treated me as her own. I never wanted for anything. I received the same treatment that her own children received. Honestly, I was one of her children because there was no differentiation between me and her biological children. Yet, I was still aching for a mother's love. And unfortunately, my mother never got well.

Fast-forward to 2012—It was Friday afternoon and I was leaving work on the way home to enjoy my weekend. My boss stopped me and said that I had a call in the office. After my "hello," my younger sister relayed the devastating news that my mother was in the hospital unresponsive and they weren't sure how long she would make it. My son and I arrived at the hospital and I witnessed my mother appearing the weakest I'd ever seen her. She was moved to the Intensive Care Unit and I was left trying to piece together what could have happened for us to be there at that bleak point. To this day I still don't know the truth.

Day and night, my siblings and I sat in the hospital watching our mother die right before our eyes. Truthfully, I don't even remember how I got to the hospital some days, or if I even went home. I am so thankful for my loving family during that time. They made sure that my son ate, that he was entertained, and that he was well.

I remember sitting by my mother's bedside and listening to "Dear Mama" by Tupac at least 40 times a day. Tears always started to fall towards the end…

> *"…I wish I could take the pain away,*
> *If you could make it through the night, there's a brighter day.*
> *Everything will be alright if you hold on;*
> *It's a struggle everyday gotta roll on.*
> *And there's no way I can pay you back,*
> *But my plan is to show you that I understand…you are appreciated."*

It wasn't until I was sitting in the hospital room that all the feelings of abandonment and rejection returned. The questions returned shortly after. *"Why did she leave me? Didn't she know I needed her? How come she didn't let me help her get better?"* I finally settled on having a woman to woman conversation with her after I had to complete the paperwork to become her Power of Attorney. Knowing that at any moment life could change, there was so much I needed to get off my chest. I know that she couldn't speak back to me but I was sure that she heard everything I said. For a while, I just sat and asked questions. *"How could you leave us like that? Did you really try to get better? What took you so long to come get me?"* A calming spirit came over me and I swear I just started hearing her speak to me. She told me that she just wanted the best for her children and she knew that she couldn't give us that. She knew that the family members that cared for us would treat us well and always be there for us. She said she was certain that she had raised strong, resilient children who could persevere through anything. I could do nothing but kiss her on her cheek and tell her thank you. She didn't personally provide me the best, but she made sure that I had it. Every family member I have stayed with since I was 14 years old treated me like one of their children, not their god-child, not their niece, or their stepdaughter. I was one of theirs. They did exactly what my mother knew they would; they raised me as their own.

I entitled this "A Mother's Love" because I know what it is like to both need it and not have it, but also to have it and not cherish it. We must cherish those women in our lives that bring us wisdom and are there to help us up when we fall. We all need those strong women in our corner to love us, hug us, and knock us down a notch when we need it. These women may not be natural mothers, but God will send you someone to love you as their own.

Dear Daddy,
Thank You for the spirit of forgiveness! I thank You for the amazing women that You have placed in my path to guide me in this journey of life. Help me to be that shining light

for someone else! In Jesus' Name, Amen!

Ladies, today I EMPOWER you to first forgive so that you can receive your healing. I EMPOWER you to recognize your blessing may not be packaged the way that you would like, but know that God is still providing and caring for you in His way. Lastly, I EMPOWER you to nurture and care for your friends, family, and the women in your lives with the touch of "A Mother's Love" that is within you.

7 DADDY ISSUES
Tiffany T. Huff

But as many as received Him, to them He gave the right to become children of God, even to those who believe in His name, who were born, not of blood nor of the will of the flesh nor of the will of man, but of God. John 1:12-13 NASB

My boys' father was murdered when they were two and four years old. My father died last January. I was thirty-five years old. When their father was murdered, I grieved. The boys grieved. We grieved. But I had no idea what it felt like to not have a father. I had no idea what it meant to my boys at their cores, to be fatherless boys at such young, tender ages.

As they have grown up over the years, we have talked and cried about the pain and anger of the void their father's absence left. I've listened to the "what ifs" created in their lives by that void. *What if Daddy were here? What if he could take us? What if we could watch? What if we could be? What if we could do? What if we could have?* What if, what if, what if... And while I feel immeasurable compassion for my boys and the mom in me wants to make it better, there's no way I could manifest those what ifs or imagine what the void felt like for them inside.

When the boys' pain and anguish showed up in overwhelming ways, I too was overwhelmed because I knew there was little I could do to soothe their aching hearts, or to reassure them the pain would ever permanently go away. I love them hard through these times, and pray even harder for and with them, and I encourage them to write out their feelings, good and bad. Sometimes though, mom just can't make it better.

But God.

My Daddy was there for my boys and I during those times. He was my best friend for thirty-five years. Even though he was getting old, I never really gave serious thought to what life would be like without him or what the void would be for me, for us. The boys spent the summers with him in North Carolina then he would come up to Pittsburgh and visit us in the fall and go back to the comforts of the south for winter. Only when he came to visit in the fall of 2014, his stay became permanent. His health suddenly began to decline at an alarmingly rapid pace.

Now, the boys and I were Grandad's care givers. Day by day and month by month we watched my Daddy fight to regain his strength, to fight the pains and infections, to hold on to his faith for a healing. His healing only came as he began to make his transition to eternity. My best friend of thirty-five years, the first man I'd ever loved, my Daddy was gone.

I've been haunted by so many questions surrounding our losses. Is it more of a tragedy to lose your father early and spend your whole life wondering what it would have been like with him in it; or is having your father for all of your life, every step of the way and then having to deal with the loss at a time in your life when you feel you need him the most more tragic? Is it a harder tragedy to bear loving your father through the pain that would ultimately consume him and stand by him up to the moment he takes his last breath, or when all of a sudden you get a call that he's been shot, and doctors tried but couldn't save him? Can the depth, or impact of tragedy even be measured?

    The truth is, the good news is both my boys and I have had a Daddy with us from the times we were formed in the womb. The truth is no matter when we lose our fathers on earth, our heavenly Father is with us every single day of our lives. He is there to comfort us, strengthen us and most importantly to love us. What God has shown me is the void of losing a loved one becomes unbearable when we focus our attention so heavily on the void itself. The moment we change our perspective and begin to focus on the impact the person has made on our lives, the moment we begin to allow God to be enough, and to truly hold on to God's promises, healing begins. Each day is a new opportunity for the boys and me to be intentional about embracing the presence of our heavenly Father and cherishing the memories we had with our daddies here on earth. Each day we get the gift of trading our Daddy issues for our crowns as sons and daughters of the king.

Dear Daddy,
Thank You for who You are and who You have always been. Thank You for loving me and for reminding me that You've adorned me with the crown as the heir and daughter of the most-high King. Thank You for reminding me that through Your grace I can wake up every day and trade my tragedy for treasure. In Jesus' Name, Amen!

Daughter of the King, I EMPOWER you to trade your daddy issues for your crown of beauty and embrace the unconditional love that can only be bestowed upon you by your heavenly Daddy.

She Has Been Where I'm Standing.

"And they have defeated him by the blood of the Lamb and by their testimony."

~Revelation 12:11 NLT

8 PEACE BY PEACE
Jennifer Anthony

For as he thinketh in the heart so is he… Proverbs 23:7 KJV

Growing up, I was such a sweet, loving and happy young girl. Somewhere in my twenties, I lost my innocence and became a Drama Queen. Over time and in my early thirties, I felt all my dreams faded away and I became bitter. It seems as if my name changed to Debbie Downer and Negative Nancy because I was walking around with so much anger.

One day I was in Walmart and ran into one of my girlfriend's 86-year-old grandad. He made the mistake of asking how I was doing and I replied, "I'm ok but…" I started rambling off everything that was going on in my life and he stopped me half way through my complaining. "I'm sorry, but you are too blessed to be stressed. And if I would have known you had a list of complaints, I would have never asked how you are doing." He gave me a hug and walked away. He probably ran away with all that I had just dumped on him! As I stood there with the "well I have never" face, something came over me. In that very moment I began to pray for peace. I needed God's perfect peace. The type of peace that is spoken of in **Philippians 4:7**. I needed peace that I couldn't even understand.

According to the word of God, the mind and spirit work together. The disappointment in myself filled my mind with reasoning and fear and that turned into anxiety and worrying. I had demonic strongholds and a lack of faith going on in my life. When things did not go my way I would fall apart, and the way I coped with my anger was through lust, pleasure and greed. I had a constant mentality battle because my actions did not align with my core values. These strongholds set up many layers of negative actions such as nit picking, being critical and judgmental. I was also extremely intolerant, frustrated and hypocritical which all had to end.

What I've learned is one of the bravest, yet hardest parts about being set free from negativism is facing the truth. I had to face the fact that I was a negative person and I needed to change. Things don't always turn out the way we want them to, but to have faith is to trust and believe in God's timing. I had to learn that my words and thoughts are important because they confirm my faith. I had to change my way of thinking, and use my words to tear down any negative thoughts that crossed my mind. Don't get me wrong; I'm human and I have my moments. I constantly have to remind myself when things don't work out that I can't fall apart. The scripture does not say all things are good, but it does say that all things work together for my good.

Learning to be happy where you are and trusting that God will always lead you to the places you need to be for your good is what this faith thing is all about.

Dear Daddy,
Thank You for Your perfect peace. Thank You for always being with me and for always being good to me even when I wasn't good to myself. Most of all Father God, thank You for Your unconditional love. In Jesus' Name, Amen!

Ladies, today I EMPOWER you to always think positively on your journey and to have no regrets even when things look bad. You become what you think so be careful of your thoughts. For life is to be enjoyed and not just endured. I EMPOWER you to seek God for that Philippians 4:7 peace. "And the peace of God, which passeth all understanding, shall keep your hearts and minds through Christ Jesus."

9 HOMELESS TO HAPPINESS
Gina M. Hall

But as for you, continue in what you have learned and have firmly believed, knowing from whom you learned it. 2 Timothy 3:14 ESV

Over the past eight years, God has been trying to get my attention causing me to do some serious soul searching. I didn't understand how I went from being a professional technical trainer to a Target Guest Service team member. I was devastated, embarrassed and depressed about losing my dream job. My family is full of educators including both of my grandmothers, my grandfather, my mother and my sister. I always said that I wouldn't become a teacher, but God had a different plan for me. I always sold the technology and used the phrase, "you will learn it, live it and love it" to describe the learning process.

I became a powerful student of God. I learned, lived and loved through many life lessons.

Lesson #1: I was happily married, then got divorced and became a single, divorced mother.

Lesson #2: My son and my daughter became my motivation, strength and salvation to embrace my new role as a single, divorced mother.

Lesson #3: I could not afford to pay the mortgage for our home, so we sold the house. I got a three-bedroom apartment for my family. For elementary school, my children attended an excellent magnet school where technology was integrated into the learning plan. When my son was ready to attend middle school, I intentionally found a rental home in a certain zip code to ensure that my children were zoned to attend an excellent middle school. The cherry on top was the rental home was only $1 more than our apartment.

Lesson #4: I transitioned from a Technical Trainer to a Management Analyst position. After one year, the Management Analyst position was eliminated from the budget due to insufficient funds. I received unemployment, but was unable to pay my rent for our rental home in the suburbs.

Lesson #5: I started working as an independent consultant and later, a proposal development manager. A close friend of our family helped me to find a new apartment. She even helped me to pay my deposit and first month's rent to qualify for the new apartment.

Lesson #6: After three months, I was terminated from my proposal development manager position and then evicted from our new apartment. My son was a college sophomore living on campus. My daughter was a high school junior. One night prior to our eviction, God spoke to me and told me that my daughter had to go live with her father so that her world would not be turned upside down. That was one of the hardest decisions that I have ever had to make, but I knew exactly what I had to do. Thus, I called her devoted father. I explained that I was packing up all of our daughter's stuff and she was temporarily coming to live full-time with him. I explained to my daughter that she would be going to live with her father and that I would be going to live with my ex-husband's sister until I found a new job and got a new apartment for us.

Lesson #7: I humbly applied for a cashier job at the Target strategically located near my daughter's high school. I drove 25 miles one way from the townhouse to Target and was using almost my entire paycheck to pay for gas.

Lesson #8: For the next two years, I lived with one of my Target team members and her boyfriend. I paid $500 for rent to sleep on the living room couch. I was extremely depressed, but was in complete denial. My daily routine consisted of working my Target shift and watching television all day. My car died one day but thankfully, I was able to drive it back to the apartment parking lot. I started taking a cab or walking on sunny days to Target.

Lesson #9: My roommate told me that I had to leave the apartment because she and her boyfriend needed privacy. I moved my clothes, which were in Target and grocery store bags, from the apartment to my car that was parked broken down in the apartment parking lot.

Lesson #10: I spent the next two nights at a hotel, had thoughts of suicide and one night even slept in my car. I couldn't commit suicide because I would never leave that heavy burden on my children's hearts. The next day, I called my mother crying uncontrollably and told her that I was officially homeless. My mother also started crying and yelling because she could not believe that I had not called her sooner. My mother called me back in ten minutes and told me that I could temporarily go live with our close family friend. My mother also told me that she would help me to get my own apartment.

While I was homeless, God never left my side and provided everything that I needed to survive. Each night, I prayed to God to help me to find a new job and to keep my son and daughter happy and healthy. I learned that I was indeed a strong, resilient woman who through the grace of God always had a safe place to rest and food to eat. Today, I have my own one-bedroom apartment which is my little piece of paradise. My home and heart are full of gratitude, love, compassion and unwavering faith. I'm seeing a therapist to treat my depression. I am happy, healthy and grateful for every step, opportunity and lesson that I have experienced in my life on my path from homeless to happiness. I truly learned, lived and loved God as He helped me work through my life lessons!

Dear Daddy,
Thank You for my life's journey of learning and living through _____ to happiness. You now have my full attention. I am learning and developing a trusting, loving relationship with You through prayer. I know that You will never leave my side or forsake me because I am Your daughter. I am blessed and inspired to continue to learn it, live it and love it as You see fit for me in my life! In Jesus' Name, Amen!

Women, today I EMPOWER you to learn God, live God and love God! Whenever you feel like you can't make it one more moment, know that God is waiting for you to reach out to Him through prayer. Once He has your full attention, you must quietly and obediently listen as He provides all that you need to survive, thrive and execute His divine plan. Then, you will start to have clarity and understand your ultimate assignment and powerful purpose. God is a loving God who will strategically and intentionally guide you from the darkness to the light. I EMPOWER you to move from your place of _____ to happiness!

10 EXEMPLIFY THE LOVE OF CHRIST
Domini Gamble

For my thoughts are not your thoughts, neither are your ways my ways, saith the Lord. For as the heavens are higher than the earth, so are my ways higher than your ways and my thoughts than your thoughts. Isaiah 55:8-9 KJV

I am a recently engaged mother of one. The man that I am soon to marry is the father of my 7-year-old daughter and we have been together 9 years. You would think adding a ring and taking the relationship to the next level would be sort of easy since we've been together so long, right? Wrong!

After I said that magic word *yes* and accepted that ring, my life took off into a whirlwind. I mean the devil came and started hitting us in ways I never expected. Now don't get me wrong, after 9 years together we've experienced our share of drama. We've had drama from baby mamas, to ex-wives, family, both of us at different times losing everything financially and so on. But this time things were different. I don't know if it was the fear of being married, or marrying the wrong man, but my anxiety level was at an all-time high. That was something that has never happened to me before. On top of that, he turned so evil on me. What should have been a joyous and happy moment in my life turned sour very quickly. I prayed and asked the Lord was this a sign not to move forward? I mean I was stuck! I was left thinking, *"This is never what I thought this experience would be like."*

I was so confused because he went all out on the proposal. The man that flew me to New York just to ask me to marry him, and who is the father of my 7-year-old, and whom I've been with for 9 years was treating me like I was the enemy! I mean screaming at me and not wanting to talk to me. He actually got up and left me during one of our pre-marital counseling sessions and said that he was done with me. I no longer knew that person, and I had NO idea where he had emerged from. I grew so unhappy; I told my planner about 4 times by then to stop planning the wedding. I needed to get before God and gain clarity on what He would have me to do next. And that is exactly what I did.

I fasted for about a month and half seeking the Lord for wisdom, clarity, knowledge—for *something*! But what I received is so not what I was expecting. Instead of God giving me the green light to run for the nearest exit as I thought and hoped He would, He instead started dealing with me, about *me*. God started showing me that I was going through a process, one that was preparing and strengthening me for this new journey that I was about to embark upon. Next, He started showing me how to act and respond in love oppose to being defensive and getting angry. Even if he's the one who's wrong… *What, really God? Are you are telling me that I have to be nice to this joker despite all the mean things that he is saying and doing to me?* "Yes," is what I heard back clear as day. That right there literally broke my spirit.

See, growing up I was always overlooked and talked down to by those closest to me. I always felt that no one ever saw me, or tried to get to know me. So now to hear the Lord say, "No, you can't leave; you must stay. If you hold on something great will come out of this," hurt me to my core. I couldn't believe that I had gone most of my life being talked down to and overlooked, and now I was going to have to accept a husband who treated me the same way. I could not understand that, let alone receive it. I didn't know how long it would be before the greatness would come and that scared me. So I fasted some more; I just knew that I was hearing was wrong. But instead of hearing 'go' like I wanted, God kept sending me to scriptures dealing with love and how to love.

Two people even came to me and said, "No matter what he does, don't you let him take you out of yourself. Don't you act unseemly. You stay Christ-like and remain true to yourself." That's Gods way of saying don't you be fussing and cussing; I don't care what he does. I heard it, but I didn't really receive it because it was going against everything that I had been taught.

"God, what are You are trying to show me?" That is when the revelation began. God was showing us both what was in us, (me the hurt from old childhood wounds and him his anger and unforgiveness) so that he could help get it out of us. The purpose was never to live with it, but to get *free* from it. I kept missing the point because my fear had me so focused on problem that I forgot the **promise.** So much so, that I purposefully shut out the voice of God, because I was so hurt that He wanted me to live (what I thought) an unhappy life.

Can I say that month was so chaotic for me? I called myself seeking out God for clarity but when it didn't align with what I wanted to hear, I became tone death. How many of us are guilty of doing just that? Picking and choosing which of God's instructions we want to obey and not obey. But by doing this we actually provide an open door for chaos and confusion to enter into our lives.

While I was going through this, I had no peace, no rest, and no joy. My hurt, disappointment, and deliberate disobedience opened the door to fear, shame, and an anxiety level that I had never experienced before. But when I surrendered all to the Lord, I immediately felt an instant peace come over me. The peace, in which I had been seeking the whole time, came when I stopped fighting and told the Lord *yes!*

Dear Daddy,
I no longer want to be out of alignment with You. Help me to let go of the issues of my past so they no longer negatively affect my future. Teach me, Lord, how to walk and respond in Your agape love, while being steadfast and unmovable in my faith trusting that You will see me through. In Jesus' Name, Amen!

Ladies, today I EMPOWER you to let go of the "what if" mentality and step out on faith by trusting in God. No longer worrying on what might be, but focused on what God said. For if He said it, will He not do it? God has already promised you the victory; I EMPOWER you to be at peace to move forward today.

11 DON'T GIVE UP NOW
Keviyona T. Ray

"And let us not grow weary of doing good, for in due season we will reap, if we do not give up." Galatians 6:9 ESV

Last year was full of highs and lows for me. One of my lowest lows was when I began pursuing the next steps in my career. I completed a professional cohort that people assured me would be a guaranteed way into an education administration position. I went to all the meetings and completed all assignments but I was not being fully attentive. Believing that I did not need to go over and beyond because I was qualified and had more experience than many of the people in the room, I knew that I would be accepted into the residency. My coach/advisor was also convinced that with my knowledge I would be accepted into the residency.

I give my all when presented with any task but that time I did not perform as myself. I was in the program because others told me, "It is a sure way in." Taking your God given gifts and talents for granted will backfire on you. Never take for granted how smart you are, how qualified you are, how much money you have, how healthy you are, or how great your marriage is because God has a way of humbling you. **"Do nothing from selfish ambition or conceit, but in humility count others more significant than yourselves. Let each of you look not only to his own interests, but also to the interests of others. Have this mind among yourselves, which is yours in Christ Jesus." Philippians 2: 3-5 ESV**

At the end of the program I received a perfect score on my project. The panel thoroughly enjoyed my presentation and again I felt like it was going to be an effortless victory. I was certain that I was going to the next level in the program. I was sure that the relationships I had built and the impressions I had made on people were a sure shot in. The fact that I was qualified and had made all these impressions on others made me think, *"Oh these people have heard about me; that's why they didn't really ask me anything."* Oh, but girl was I wrong!

Everyone begin receiving their acceptance letters and I was denied. Denied! *"Try again next year,"* with little other explanation. I tried to walk around pretending that I wasn't fazed by saying things such as "I'm good! I didn't want this internship anyway." In reality, I was deeply devastated. No one could really understand why I did not receive the internship; everyone was shocked. I usually have crazy faith but I found myself saying, "God has something better; this was not for me," and struggling to truly embrace that declaration. I felt like a complete failure.

The summer came and people began requesting my resume` and setting up interviews. After my initial disappointment with the internship, I really thought one of the interviews would pan out great. I was thinking, "The internship was not for me because this is it!" Again, I received not one, but three denials! The interesting thing is that during that time, I called in all my prayer warriors, I began seeking God and decided that I was done trying because I could not take any more rejection.

Always be careful what you ask for! Rejection began coming in every area of my life. It was to the point that I was even rejected for a summer school position. How pathetic is that?! An interview is not even required to teach summer school, so you can see why I was beyond devastated. Everyone was still trying to encourage me, but I did not want to hear any of it. I felt like a failure. Have I said that a few times already? *"God usually hears me; why isn't He listening? Why had He not answered me? Why did He let me get humiliated in front of my peers?"* I was really perplexed.

Now that you have received the narrative, let me explain the turning point and why I composed this EmpowerMoment. Being taught all my life that failure was not an option sure was not at the forefront of my thoughts. I felt like a failure. But there's no surprise there! Accepting the fact that everything that I had worked for over a decade would not come to fruition was a tough pill to swallow, but I convinced myself that it was okay. Mediocrity had never been an option in my life, but I was going to accept it.

Just when I thought all that I would ever be was a Literacy Coach--which, by the way, is an awesome job--God sent an angel. My job as a Literacy Coach is a very big deal but I was too pre-occupied looking for something else. One day while I was working my summer security job--(Yes, you read that right! *My. Summer. Security. Job!*)--my administrator approached me with tears welling in her eyes. She discussed the school's reading scores from the district's assessment. She explained that as a result of my training, support, resources and the mere fact that I was a part of the team, my school had achieved record breaking gains. That information was exactly what I needed to get my head back in the game. I no longer felt like a failure because I had truly achieved success!

Going to my secret place and consulting God is something that I do often. My secret place is wherever I can spend time praying and conversing with God. During those devastating moments, I found myself living in my secret place. It was there that He revealed so many profound things to me. I had become arrogant. I forgot to consult Him about all my decisions. I began listening to others. I was looking for approval from man. I was denied access to something I felt I deserved. And of course I felt like a failure. However, God restored my joy but it didn't come packaged the way that I thought it would.

Dear Daddy,

Thank You for allowing Your grace and mercy to protect and sustain me. Thank You for not allowing me to give up. God, continue to send reminders when I am not depending solely on You. Continue to humble me when I forget that all things work together for my good. In Jesus' Name, Amen!

Women of God, I EMPOWER you to never forget that God is your source. Always remember that nothing is too hard for Him. When man/woman says no, God has already said yes to something else. When you feel like the world is against you, I EMPOWER you to remember that God is with you. Never become so consumed with fame, money, status or titles that you forget that God is the reason. Failing does not make you a failure and losing does not make you a loser. Don't give up now!

12 NO PRESSURE, NO DIAMOND
Keena Miquel Jordan

**And we know that all things work together for good to them that love God, to them who are the called according to his purpose.
Romans 8:28 KJV**

    A few years ago, I found myself in a situation where I was working with someone who drove me crazy. She initially seemed to be a very nice lady who was fun, giving and easy to talk to. I really believed it would turn into a solid friendship. But as time went on something wasn't quite right. She kept doing things that left me in a constant state of confusion and agitation. One day we got along great while enjoying a meal at a fabulous restaurant, the next day she treated me like a high school rival. Or I'd be searching for an item that no one could explain the disappearance of, only to discover that she had it at her home the entire time. Some days we were good and some I couldn't wait to get out of there. It was a stressful environment to say the least. My clients were starting to notice the tension. At one point I knew I had to leave for my own sanity or else someone was going to get beat down!

    Many nights I would leave work and question why I was being treated so badly. *"What did I do to deserve this? I don't bother anyone. Is it just me Lord? Maybe I'm the crazy one."* I began to doubt myself and wonder what was wrong with me, especially since she was very nice and loving *at times*. I loved my work place but I didn't enjoy working with that lady. I truly felt like I was being tortured. I remember crying out to the Lord. *"Why is this so hard? Why am I here? HELP!"*

    Sometimes in life we go through storms and we have to deal with difficult people (coworkers, family members, spouses, etc.) God will let us stay in those uncomfortable situations and He will allow people to treat us poorly in order to shift something inside of us. It is all about transforming and refining us into the women that He created us to be. Without the pressures of life, we can never be fully developed into our diamond status. Intolerable circumstances can strengthen and show us how to love people unconditionally. We are all God's children. You never know what the story is behind a person's negative behavior. This does not give you the thumbs up to stay in physically or emotionally abusive situations. However, God is aware of some things that you may be enduring and if you trust Him, He will surely bless and favor you right in their face! Weeping may endure for a night but joy most definitely comes in the morning!

Dear Daddy,
There's a battle going on inside of me but I thank You for not placing more on me than I can bear. Please help me to leave vengeance to You. Help me to turn my trials into testimonies. Change me Lord. Make me better and not bitter. Give me the strength and tenacity to handle whatever comes my way. In the midst of trouble, I know You are already there. Let Your will reign supreme! In Jesus Name, Amen!

Diamonds in the Making, I EMPOWER you today to stay strong in the midst of adversity. Don't repay evil with evil; treat all people with love even when they're undeserving. I EMPOWER you to trust God no matter the circumstances. Trust that His process of pressure is transforming you into the most beautiful diamond. Ask that He go before you in trying situations and be patient as He prepares your way of escape. God is all-knowing and all-powerful. Nothing is too hard for Him. His love is everlasting and infinite. If He be for us, who can be against us?

13 IN AN INSTANCE
Harriet Noel Jones

For our light affliction, which is but for a moment, worketh for us a far more exceeding and eternal weight of glory; While we look not at the things which are seen, but at the things which are not seen: for the things which are seen are temporal; but the things which are not seen are eternal. 2 Corinthians 4:17-18 KJV

On December 5, 2014 in the wee hours of the morning, I gave the love of my life, my best friend, my man of God, my husband of thirty-three years, his last breath and he gave me his. He transitioned from this life to his eternal life in an instance and suddenly my life was forever changed. His transition swiftly catapulted me from wife to widow.

In an instance, April 11, 2014, the hospital room was very still as the veil of death was slowly masking his eyes. With spiritual authority, I called him back to life in this realm; the veil retreated and the story began. My husband suffered three brain bleeds due to heparin therapy and was placed in intensive care. Multiple units of blood were given to reverse the blood thinning and stop the bleeding. He was placed in a drug induced coma and on life support.

In an instance, I girded up the loins of my mind, silenced all of the other voices that spoke death and I spoke life indeed. To satan I said, "*No deal,*" and quickly brought my emotions into check and under subjection to the obedience of Christ. Walking through the most critical challenge of our lives, I rolled the cares on the Lord and stood firm against the pressure from the physicians. They strongly advised me to pull the plug and let him go because his prognosis was poor at best. He was fast approaching death but if he survived, a vegetative state would be inevitable.

In an instance, believing God's promises, I witnessed, against all odds, as my best friend miraculously walked out of the hospital and rehabilitation. He left the wheel chair and the walker behind, returned to church, performed a wedding and even drove on the interstate again.

In an instance, October 25, 2014, the enemy launched another attack attempting a repeat of April, but it was still no deal. The symptoms implicated another brain bleed but all of the results indicated no additional damage and he walked out again.

In an instance, three days after his heaven declaration, the first hours before dawn, peace entered the room. With his final exhales, time and the forces of darkness stood at attention in homage as the man of God took his flight into eternal glory.

In an instance, on that day, I inquired of the Lord for answers. So many miracles had manifested and God had done everything that I asked.

God responded in an instance. *This time I did what He asked.*

In an instance, my heavenly Father gently assured me that because of my faithfulness, He would be my keeper and guide. One instance led to another instance and now more than two years later, God has been true to His word. He has kept me, carried me, shielded me, and provided for me without grief. You see He reminded me that because Jesus has borne our griefs and sorrows, I did not have to bear them. I not only survived, I thrived…in an instance.

Dear Daddy,
Thank You that in life's instances, You are always with me. You never leave me and You never forsake me. I praise You that my instances are just for a moment and have an expiration date. Help me to view my instances as the light and temporary situations that they are. Continue to remind me that though they are momentary, they work for my good and Your glory. Strengthen me to trust that with every instance, You have already planned a way of escape for me to bear them. In Jesus' Name, Amen!

Ladies, I EMPOWER you to value your instances as opportunities for increase in spiritual maturity. They allow you to grow in the Lord. Be transparent and use them as a platform that others may comprehend the power of God operating in your life. And as they look at you, they see the Father. Take your focus off the temporary instances and put it on the eternal God.

14 IT'S A JOURNEY; SEEK GOD THROUGH IT!
Sherita Redmond-Yamini

**But he said to me, "My grace is sufficient for you, for my power is made in perfect weakness." Therefore, I will boast all the more gladly about my weakness, so that Christ's power may rest on me.
2 Corinthians 12:9 NIV**

Growing up in the Woodlawn Community of Chicago during the 80's was quite like the world we live in today, with the exception of social media. It was dangerous and overturned by poverty, the "Crack Era," gang wars, where shots rang out in the middle of the day, as children were walking home from school and children were raising themselves or at home with their grandparents. Those experiences were traumatizing to me at such a ripe age and I remember them vividly. However, what I remember most clearly are the horrifying experiences that I experienced right in my own home.

I suffered grave emotional and physical abuse from my mother from birth until the age of 6 years old. She didn't want me and she hated me. My father sold drugs out of our home, he beat my mother all of the time, and got her addicted to crack cocaine. As a result of that atmosphere, I never saw my own face in the mirror until I reached the age of 30 years old.

As a child, my mother beat me daily with her fist, objects, and picked my small frame up by the neck and choked me into unconsciousness in front of the bathroom mirror. She had the voice of a demon as she assured me that she wanted me to watch myself die. Threatening me that if I ever told, she would kill me. Well, I woke up in the hospital, just to see her face taking me back home. She broke my spirit for all women, used fear to keep me silent, and most of all ate my identity like a hungry, roaring lion. One day, I ran to my grandmother's house a block away in my underwear and no shoes and I told her everything.

She immediately began to pray and made me repeat every word. She taught me how to pray and at that very moment God broke my silence. From that day I prayed all day. In the store, while driving, everywhere. People thought I was insane, but I didn't care. I was talking to God, who takes care of His children. I was so grateful that He left me in the care of my loving grandmother from that day forward.

The onset of sexual molestation for me was at the age of ten. Living in the home with my grandparents who came from a small town in Mississippi, were uneducated and accustomed to sexual sin being a normal way of life, made my allegations pretty worthless. When I finally told what had happened to me, I was a bit older. My grandmother was crushed and compassionate. However, my grandfather told me that in South "stuff" like that happened and now I was old enough and had permission to be a "fass tail." I died! My soul died in that moment. It was so real that I saw my spirit leave my body as I watched myself run away. For years I was traumatized as I was drugged with alcohol and narcotics. I was a child. A very broken child. I was lost somewhere deep in a generational curse.

Being raised by dysfunctional human beings could have morphed me into a dysfunctional person. If your parents were raised to be absent, abusive, narcissistic, addicts, sexual adulterers, pedophiles and were uneducated, homeless, unaware of mental illness or lived in poverty, you would have generations of strong spirits to fight. Well that is where I found myself. How did I get through? Glad you asked!

I learned to study the Bible, pray and became active in church. I focused hard in school and engaged in arts and sports as an outlet. Those things gave me peace, got me into college and laid the foundation for my future career. What I learned is that I had to go through those things, so I took God with me everywhere I had to go. I was willing to do what He told me, so I asked. God ordered my steps; He was my light in such a dark place. His unconditional love and His grace transformed me in His image. Sometimes God won't deliver you from your mess, but He will be with you in it. Everything that you are currently dealing with can be used by God for His purposes. It may not feel great, but trust that He is preparing you for something greater. This is your journey; seek God through it!

Dear Daddy,
I don't want to live another day of my life in dysfunction. I choose You, God, to transform me because I can't do it on my own. I know that my circumstances do not define me, but that You can use them for Your purposes. Starting right now, help me to put my trust in You and learn Your word, so that You may live through me. Fill me with Your love and give me everlasting life. In Jesus' Name Amen!

Women, today I EMPOWER you to take your journey and seek God through it. You may feel like your situation is less than ideal but God can help you and wants to help you. I EMPOWER you to yield to Him so that He can heal your heart and change your circumstances.

God's Got Me!

"Never will I leave; never will I forsake you."

~Hebrews 13:5 NLT

15 BE ANXIOUS FOR NOTHING
Ana M. Jackson

Be anxious for nothing, but in everything by prayer and supplication with thanksgiving, let your request be made known to God, and the peace of God, which surpasses all understanding, will guard your hearts and mind through Christ Jesus. Philippians 4:6-7 NKJV

We tend to personally get anxious, worried and distracted by life experiences that don't go the way we planned. It's often difficult to sit still and be at peace when it appears that all hell is breaking out around you. You may have gotten a bad report from the doctor, your job may be on the line, bills piling up or even your relationship is rocky. How many of you can attest to at least one of these things? Me too girlfriend! I have been there and experienced ALL of them, but God! I want to share one of my favorite scriptures that I recite when trouble tends to brew. **"No weapon that is formed against thee shall prosper..." (Isaiah 54:17)** This scripture will never leave my heart because my mom recited it to me every time I rang her phone with disturbing news.

I am a parent to a total of 5 beautiful children; I have 3 that I naturally gave birth to. Before I remarried, it was just my 3 babies and me and we lived 700 miles away from my family. I can honestly say that we encountered many things that would naturally shake the earth's foundation and could have pushed me to having a breakdown, but God!

In my life experiences, I was laid off a couple times, car repossessed a few times and had to move from a beautiful 4-bedroom home that I had built to a 3-bedroom apartment in a neighborhood that wasn't my heart's desire but where I could afford. After we were finally settled, I found myself unemployed *again* due to the economy taking a turn. This time, I was blessed to be granted the opportunity to continue to live in my apartment by working on the complex grounds as the Pool Monitor. In the beginning, I was ashamed to do such a task, but if Mary Magdalene (in Luke 7:36) could begin to use her tears to wash Jesus' feet and dry them with her hair, who am I to be so prideful? I wiped my tears and toted my kids right along with me to the pool. Wow, that was a very humbling experience for an educated person who worked as an accountant and I was truly grateful. But God!

Why am I sharing this with you? Because I want you to know that God never left me nor forsook me in any of my trials and tribulations and that forced me to be anxious for nothing. I found myself in a predicament of having to keep looking for a job over and over again. My fiancé at the time (who is now my husband) told me something that I will never forget.

He said, *"You are going to keep repeating the same test over and over again until you pass it. Don't expect God to promote you to the next level until you master where you are."* Ouch! I had to seriously examine myself and make some changes. As uncomfortable as that was, I did it because I was determined to pass the test!

In **MATTHEW 6:31-32,** it says, **"Therefore take no thought, saying, What shall we eat? Or What shall we drink? Or Wherewithal shall we be clothed? (For all these things do the Gentiles seek) for your heavenly Father knows that you have need of these things.**

Through my whole ordeal, my electricity was never disconnected, my kids were clothed and we never missed a meal. Eventually, I was blessed with a better paying job, with a better vehicle, and was able to move back into another home! Isn't God good?! Were there moments that I felt dismayed? Absolutely. However, I knew who my Daddy was and He is the King that sits high and looks low and my provider!

In my times of waiting on God I had to find peace. Here are a few tips I would like to share with you on finding peace.

- Let go of the things you cannot change.
- Learn to be quiet and still.
- Release your worries to God and sleep with a peaceful mind.
- During your daily activities, start memorizing uplifting scriptures. This positive pattern will help you train your consciousness.
- Think positively, speak favorably and act peacefully.
- Remove toxic things from your life.

Sisters, while you are in your waiting period, don't give up. God hears your prayers and He is listening and in His timing, you will be rewarded. You may not always get the answers that you want, but be obedient to His command. Trust me; you don't want to repeat the lesson over. Remember that God is allowing these things to grow your character and see how you will respond. Prove to Him that you truly live for Him and trust His plan for your life. Be anxious for nothing for God has it all under control.

Dear Daddy,
I know that You don't give me more than I can bear. If I begin to feel that way, perhaps I am leaning too much on my own power and need to become more dependent upon You. In the midst of my trials, fill me up with more of You and less of me. Help me to hear Your voice and not my own so my actions line up according to Your word and promises. In Jesus' Name, Amen!

Queens, today I EMPOWER you to take a moment to breathe and know that God is the author and the finisher of all things. Regardless

of what you see with your carnal eye, everything will turn out in your favor if you place your trust in Him. I EMPOWER you to release anything that is hindering you from getting your blessing today.

16 TOY GUNS ARE HARMLESS
Kristen R. Harris

"No weapon formed against you shall prosper, and every tongue which rises against you in judgment You shall condemn…" Isaiah 54:17 NKJV

I am totally against guns, so much that I won't even allow my children to play with toys gun of any type. They can't touch BB guns, plastic GI Joe guns, not even water guns. I just don't want them to get the idea that aiming a weapon at someone is fun and games. Because I never purchase toy guns, I've never had to address the issue until they received a water gun as a gift. Of course I allowed them to graciously accept the gift but when we returned home, I explained to them why I would have to confiscate the toy. Naturally, the inquisitive wheels of my girls' minds started turning. My eldest daughter rebuttal was simply, "But why can't we use it? It's just a fake weapon; it can't really hurt anyone!" And that innocent response from my then 7-year-old is where today's EmpowerMoment was birthed.

There are probably not too many mature believers that don't know the words that lie in **Isaiah 54:17**. If you start the scripture off with the first two words, most can recite the rest of the scripture. But how many people truly *believe* the words that they have committed to memory?

What is a weapon as it pertains to your life? The very thing that you are facing right now that has you feeling like you won't make it. Maybe your weapon is on the scale of a water gun and you are dodging squirts of family issues. Possibly your weapon is a bit grander like a BB gun and you're exhausted from ducking out of the way of pellets of unemployment and financial woes. Perhaps you're actually at war with a real weapon and the rifle is letting off bullets of pain, embarrassment and condemnation from your past. Or are you are dealing with heavy artillery and an automatic assault weapon is firing continuous shots of self-esteem, sexuality issues, depression, and suicide? Regardless of what type of weapon the adversary has engaged on your life, the Commander in Chief has sent me right to your battlefield with this very important message: **IT WON'T WORK!**

The weapons may appear to be deadly, but just as my daughter reminded us, they're fake and won't really hurt you! You are more than a conqueror in Christ Jesus! The battle is fixed and regardless of what type of big guns that devil pulls out, he loses in the end. The ducking and dodging is simply building your endurance, and God has promised that if you stay in the fight and trust Him, the victory is yours! **"These things I have spoken to you, that in Me you may have peace. In the world you will have tribulation; but be of good cheer, I have overcome the world." John 16:33 NKJV**

Even after my daughter's compelling argument, I didn't change my mind and allow them to play with the guns. However, now every time that I see one I will remember one key fact. The weapons that the enemy tries to annihilate me with are just as fake and ineffective as the toy water guns sold at the dollar store! Now that's something to get excited about!

Dear Daddy,
I thank You that every weapon that the enemy has designed to kill me has already been rendered harmless by You! When I am in the midst of a fiery attack, please remind me that the battle has already been won and Your team is victorious! Help my actions to reflect that I truly believe what I read in Isaiah 54:17. In Jesus' Name, Amen!

Ladies, today I EMPOWER you to truly believe that every attack that has been launched on your life is indeed harmless. I EMPOWER you to treat every weapon—sickness, depression, death, fear, poverty, loneliness, etc.—like a toy gun made for kids. Remember NO weapon formed against you shall prosper!

I LOVE Me!

"Beauty is when you can appreciate yourself. When you love yourself, that's when you're most beautiful."

~Zoe Kravitz

17   ENOUGH IS ENOUGH…YOU ARE ENOUGH!
Marnaé A. Thompson

For you created my inmost being; you knit me together in my womb. I praise you because I am fearfully and wonderfully made; your works are wonderful, I know that full well. Psalm 139:13-14 NIV

"That's why you ain't got no daddy." "Yo mama a crackhead." "Ugh, why yo hair so nappy?" "Light Bright." "She ain't got no booty." "You ain't got no money." "That lil' job ain't nothing." "College?! Ha, Who gone pay for that?!" "Why you in school so long?" "You ain't graduated yet?" "You ain't bought no house yet?" "You ain't got no man yet?

Sound familiar? Well, it sure sounds familiar to me. These phrases were on replay in my mind for a long time. This is only a limited list of the conscious and subconscious attempts others made to destroy my self-esteem. Beginning in early childhood, we are teased and taunted about our appearance and socioeconomic status. It sounds harmless to many in the Black community because this rhetoric has been normalized. But enough is enough and I need you to understand that YOU ARE ENOUGH!

For most, the malnourishment of our self-esteem begins in the home. The destruction of our psyche continues in grade school and precedes us throughout our adulthood. As Black children we are forced into believing that we aren't and will never be "enough" for this world. We are told that our parents are failures, we aren't physically attractive, we aren't smart enough, we're unworthy of love, and financial stability isn't obtainable. Regardless of how these messages are packaged, our parents, siblings and peers are the messengers. They certainly delivered those messages to me. My siblings constantly called me names such as 'White girl" and "monkey" because of my fair skin and full features. My mother *was* a crackhead. And, I did take forever to graduate college. But guess what? I graduated!

The dialogue with those closest to us plays the largest roles in the development of our self-esteem. As a culture, we insult one another then exclaim that "it was just a joke." If you look a little deeper you'll discover that our verbiage is a direct reflection of our own self-worth or lack thereof. Realistically, we *know* that that rhetoric is a deliberate attempt to tear down and/or stunt the confidence of our counterparts. For many, the struggle to discover self-worth continues to be a pitfall, thus resulting in long-term destructive behavior.

Well, today, I'm here to tell you that YOU ARE ENOUGH! As stated throughout the entire Bible, God created you in His own image. We've all stumbled. Heck, most of us have not only stumbled but we've fallen face first into a pile of cow dung! But guess what? Every stain can be washed away. God's grace and mercy is sufficient. His sweet and glorious blood washes every one of our inequities away.

Whether you struggle with generational curses such a promiscuity, substance abuse, or financial ruin; whether you've created your own struggles such as job loss or resisting to grow; whether someone stole your innocence through lying, cheating, sexual assault, or theft--God is with you. He knows that you have the potential to be exactly who He created you to be. Think about it. God created you! You were *created*! What an honor! God thought that someone like you was necessary. So, He *made* you! You have a specific role to play in this thing called life. Trust Him and His works!

There are some cruel people in this world. Many of those cruel people are people that you call friend or family. Yet, they are an intricate part of your life's story. They are necessary for your growth. All of the negative connotations, all of the pain, all of the self-esteem killers, all of the dream snatchers, all of the innocence stealers are a part of your story. Your story was designed to catapult you into greatness. Your road to greatness is what is going to change your life and the lives of those around you. You have the power to shape generations to come.

Naysayers will always abound. Take refuge in knowing that God gave you the tools and wherewithal to be great! Every kink on your head, every love handle, every twang in your voice, every failed course, every financial misstep, every frustration, every disappointment, every missed opportunity, every moment of doubt will all lead to your destiny. You were created to impact lives. You are more powerful than you have ever imagined. You were created *on purpose*. You were beautifully and wonderfully made. You have always been and will always be enough!

Dear Daddy,

Thank You for reminding me that I was created in Your image. Thank You for reminding me that regardless of what others have said to me and about me, I am perfect in Your eyes. I now understand that family and friends may not have the capacity to properly love me. I ask that You continue to be a constant source of love and confidence for me. I ask that You hold my hand and support me when I struggle with my self-worth. I ask that You restore all that was stolen from me, including my innocence. I ask that You continue to build me up so that I can confidently do Your will. In Jesus' Name, Amen!

Ladies, today I EMPOWER you to love yourself unconditionally, wholeheartedly with flaws and all. Love yourself. Often times we seek validation from all of the wrong sources. Today, I EMPOWER you to take ownership of your shortcomings, perfection and power.

You are more than enough. There is nothing that anyone can say or do that has the authority to break you. You have the power to manifest all of the desires of your heart. Knowledge of thyself is powerful and you've got the power.

18 SELF LOVE = SELF CONFIDENCE
Tanika McBee

For the Lord shall be thy confidence and shall keep thy foot from being taken. Proverbs 3:26 KJV

As a woman, you are equipped with confidence. In order to set your confidence free, you have to love yourself and put your trust in God. We must be assertive but remain humble. Have just enough faith to believe that you can rely on the gifts God has given you. Learn how to appreciate your own qualities and abilities without waiting on validation from man or *a man*. Besides, you can't love anyone else truthfully if you don't love yourself. Yes, you will get weak! When you do, fall to your knees, pray and remember that strength and confidence already lies within you, so release it!

The idea of being able to write a letter to my younger self is captivating; if I only knew then what I know now! Before the Lord saved me, I was a mess and didn't even know it. Of course I'm not perfect now, but in comparison of the two, I'll take the latter version of me. As a young lady, I wasn't horrible but I was lost. I performed well in elementary school and overall I wasn't labeled as a "bad kid." However, as I grew into my teenage years things changed. Not having a father in my life, I looked for that love in the wrong places and ended up turning to the street life. Even through her own struggles, I still believe my mommy did considerably well with my brother and me. My family collectively helped to take care of me. My grandmother was the matriarch, my four uncles were the male figures I looked to and then my grandfather was the stern provider. With that, there was still a void. There is just something about a father's love that a girl needs to learn how she should be loved and in turn how to love herself. Always longing for that love and affection that I felt was missing, I sought attention from my relationships emotionally and physically.

Seeking validation and not knowing how to fully love myself tampered with my self-confidence and caused fear to set in. I was fearful of becoming the woman my Father in heaven created me to be. Yes, I was given the word early, my very own Bible, at the age of twelve. I was bred from a family of believers on both sides, true men and women of faith. Yet, I didn't always stick with Him. However, even when I strayed from the Lord's will, I always felt Him surrounding me and pulling me closer to Him. For a long time, I didn't love myself enough to care about the situations I put myself in, but thankfully my Father in heaven did. He saved me from myself and He kept me from so much hurt, harm and danger. Today, I am much wiser and walk boldly in my confidence but I am thankful that He still keeps His angels encamped around me and extends His grace and mercy to me daily.

Let us begin today to love ourselves enough and care enough to know who we are and whose we are. Understanding your own capabilities and character will maximize your feelings of self-worth. As much effort as we put into that person we love or that career that makes us money, we need to put into ourselves. Have compassion for you! Self-compassion and self-appreciation are real. Be kind to yourself and appreciate who God made you to be. When you know your worth they will too!

When you undervalue what you do, the world will undervalue who you are.
~Oprah Winfrey

Don't beat yourself up about past mistakes, they were needed to mature and mold you. Don't let what you feel are personal inadequacies overshadow your personal triumphs. Consider yourself as a pearl, which is a precious stone made by pain and suffering that comes to be rare, fine and valuable in the end. As I mentioned before, remain humble in all you do but know that you have enough God-given love within you and enough strength to build the confidence that will carry you throughout this lifetime.

Dear Daddy,
Thank You for being an awesome God! Thank You for loving me enough to equip me with everything I need to fulfill the works You have set forth for me. I know what I've been through was necessary and I'm grateful for it. Please forgive me for not loving myself enough to use the gifts You have given me. Forgive me for not having confidence in myself and therefore not having confidence in You. Lord, endow me with Your spirit and continue to strengthen me. In Jesus' Name, Amen!

Confident Women, I EMPOWER you to let your issues, your inadequacies and your struggles act as building blocks for your tower of confidence. It lies within you, so be fearless and courageous in all you do. Love yourself and know that your Father in heaven has already equipped you with everything you need to survive this moment in time called life. I love you!

19 GOD'S MARVELOUS WORKS
LaVonna V. Fields

I praise You, for I am fearfully and wonderfully made; Marvelous are Your works, And that my soul knows very well. Psalm 139: 14 NKJV

On Wednesday, January 4, 2017, I turned 40 years old. On that day, I stood unclothed and looked at myself in a full-sized mirror. Everything I took note of, did not look like the 20-year-old me that I mentally see when I close my eyes. I have smile lines and hair that grows on my face that was not there before. I have roundness and slopes on my body that used to be fine lines and curves. I also begin that long list of comparisons to pictures of women that are posted all throughout social, print and televised media. *Are my thighs shapely like so and so is? If I hold in my stomach, could I wear the dress that Jane Doe did in that magazine spread?*

I also compare myself to other women by thinking *"least I am not as big as her."* This "mean girl" confidence builder only works for a few seconds because I then see another woman who has a "better figure" than me and then I am once again faced with my own body insecurities. These insecurities have kept me from going on outings with my family. For example, last summer I refused to go to a theme park because I was afraid that I was too heavy to get on any of the rides. Therefore, I lied and stated that I no longer was interested in riding the roller coasters, so I did not go. I have also declined family trips to the water parks because I do not want anyone to see me in a swim suit. These thoughts even cripple my mind into thinking that I am not sexy or small enough to be intimate with my husband.

While looking in the mirror that day, I recalled my favorite scriptures: **Psalm 139:14**. I began to think about the words of David's Psalm and then the words fearfully and wonderfully made popped into my mind. I had to stop and realize that I have taken for granted this earthly body that God has blessed me with. It must have grieved God to hear my negative thoughts about His marvelous work. Therefore, I began to praise God for everything this aging body has allowed me to do over the last 40 years.

Hands: I looked at my hands and noticed that yes, they looked older; however, I used them to comfort my children and my husband with a gentle rub on their backs after a long difficult day. I also used these hands to crochet many garments that have given my family and friends warmth in cold weather. But most important, I have used my hands to lift them up in praise, prayer and a sign of surrender to our Heavenly Father's will.

Face: I stared long and hard at my face and noticed that the new lines that I currently have developed are not frowns and frustration creases. My facial lines are from smiling and laughter that I have shared with others over the forty years of my life. I also thank God that I still had my vision to read and study His word.

Body Shape: My full-figure size successfully brought three wonderful gifts from God into my life; with all three births, I was able to work all the way to each due date without complications. This body has also given me the ability to praise the Lord in dance and has laid prostrate in reverence and prayer to the Lord in worship.

There are other examples that I can give about other parts of my body that I would look at in a negative way or feel ashamed, because I don't look the way the world says I should. Now, I see myself how God sees me. I praise the Lord because I am a unique individual. I praise the Lord because I am fearfully and wonderfully made. Do you know that I hold my head higher and I have an enduring confidence that no one can take away because I am who God says I am? I encourage all of my sisters to understand your worth through God's words and praise Him because His work is marvelous. Know in your soul that you are an awesome creation of God.

Dear Daddy,
Your works are marvelous throughout the heavens and the earth. Please forgive me for my negative thoughts about the body You have created just for me. I praise You because I am fearfully and wonderfully made. And I thank You for Your marvelous work, which is me. In Jesus' Name, Amen!

Women of God, I EMPOWER you today to love yourself and to let go of all the negative thoughts regarding your body. I EMPOWER you to know in your soul that your body was created especially for you by our loving heavenly Father to live out His purpose for your life.

The Son Has Set Me Free!

"So if the Son sets you free, you will be free indeed."

~John 8:36 NIV

20 DEFINING MOMENTS
Natalie K. Byrd

Then Jesus stood up again and said to the woman, "Where are your accusers? Didn't even one of them condemn you?" "No, Lord," she said. And Jesus said, "Neither do I. Go and sin no more."
John 8:10-11 NLT

I believe a defining moment is a specific event in our life that is orchestrated to give us an opportunity to unfold a greater essence of who we are created to be. These moments unveil a unique quality within us that we've never before experienced. The trouble is, or so it seems, that defining moments are often experienced in the context of pain, rather than joy and bliss.

You should be ashamed…You're so stupid and no one wants you…You deserve to be alone… God is punishing you for your sins.

These are the words that played over and over in my mind as I sat alone in the dark in my college dorm room. I found out that I was pregnant the month before and it was turning out to be one of the most painful experiences of my life. My mother was crushed by the news and uncertain of my future, the father of my child asked me to consider abortion, I was urged to stay away from my cousin in whom I wanted to take refuge, and when word got to the mother of my roommate she found her another place to live.

I was so terribly consumed by the negative words and actions of those who knew of my pregnancy that all I could contemplate was suicide. I knew I had made a bad decision. I knew this wasn't supposed to happen, but the pressure of people's words and the burden of their actions, especially while I was hundreds of miles away from home, seemed like too much to bear. So I made a decision. I decided to go to sleep and never wake up to the pain again.

As I held pills in my hand, the life growing within me summoned me toward a different choice – to live. That night, I told myself that I would not try to *convince* anyone that I would accomplish my goals; I was going to *show* them! From there I went on a quest to prove my worth and to prove all of them wrong. I completed the semester, gave birth to my son, worked full time, and attended school full-time. By the time my son was out of preschool, I graduated college with honors. I refused to accept government help. I got married, purchased a home, opened a shelter for pregnant and parenting teenagers, started a business, earned a Master's Degree, obtained a ministerial license, served the poor, became a speaker and presenter, and served God to my fullest capacity.

Ultimately, my critics spoke differently about me. It felt good to gain the security of other people's opinion, but their acceptance came at a price. The cost was not knowing how to take refuge in God's security and acceptance alone. Underneath my accomplishments, I still felt lonely, fearful and ashamed. Although I no longer recited my suicidal mantra in the dark of the night, part of my soul still lived in the darkness of that dorm room. My defining moment – the moment that held an opportunity for me to become more of who I am, essentially trapped me in inauthentic behavior for 18 years of my life – all because of my decision to defend myself and prove others wrong.

In **John 8**, the woman caught in adultery is literally thrown into a defining moment. She knows that death is the penalty for her sin and was being dragged into the street to face her sentence publicly. Jesus' response, His defense of her, reveals three foundational principles upon which defining moments are built.

1. Jesus freed her from the judgment of others: **Where are your accusers?** I believe Jesus asked her about her accusers so that she could draw meaning from her own observation – there were none. This interaction assures us that we can live free of others' accusations. Even when words of judgment and strong opinion come, our internal freedom can be our guide toward this truth.
2. He blessed her with forgiveness and love: **Neither do I condemn you.** A woman walking away from stoning after being caught in the very act of adultery didn't happen in the culture of that day. Jesus didn't come in alignment with what culture said; He came in alignment with the Father's heart. We can rest in the sanctuary of God's love and forgiveness even after sin.
3. Jesus called her to live in greater possibility: **Go and sin no more.** Jesus presented her with the possibility to live beyond the sin of adultery. Defining moments call us to live more aligned with our true self and a higher version of the self. They invite us to pause and take a deeper look at our hearts while presenting new possibilities for our future.

Dear Daddy,
Please give me the spiritual eyes to see how You are unveiling Your identity in me. Grant me the courage to live outside my own boundaries and walk in the essence of who You created me to be. Help me open my heart to forgiveness and love and allow me to live fully in the possibilities You present in every defining moment. In Jesus' Name, Amen!

Ladies, I EMPOWER you to live free from other people's opinions and receive the blessing of forgiveness and love in your darkest moments. I EMPOWER you to break through old perceptions and past rejections to allow each defining moment to cause you to walk in the fullness of its possibility.

21 HE IS NOT A TIT FOR TAT GOD!
Chanceé Lundy

Who is a God like you, who pardons sin and forgives the transgression of the remnant of his inheritance? You do not stay angry forever but delight to show mercy. You will again have compassion on us; you will tread our sins underfoot and hurl all our iniquities into the depths of the sea. Micah 7: 18-19 NIV

"When the good Lord says so." "All in His timing." Honey, these sayings flew out of my mouth so fast it was if I had them on standby just in case someone asked me about a baby. Outwardly, I professed my faith in God and in His timing; but, inside I was full of doubt. *"God, when will it be my turn?" "Please forgive me Jesus!"* All I wanted was a child to call my own. In my early twenties, I wanted ten children but in my mid-thirties I found myself begging God to please just let me have one.

I convinced myself that God was punishing me for my disobedience. My heart ached and I felt tormented inside. God had given me a few clear directions in my life and I blatantly disregarded them in favor of what felt right to me. I disobeyed because I didn't put my complete trust in Him. He said go left and I would shift just a little bit right. He said go here and I would wander off to there. Now, I felt like I was paying the ultimate price for years of disobedience. You can relate, can't you?

My husband and I prayed for a child all the time. Heck, I even had girlfriends petitioning God on my behalf. Many times, I felt like I was going through the "prayer motions" while holding doubt in my heart. I repeatedly asked God to forgive me for not following His instruction, but the truth is I hadn't forgiven myself.

One day, I decided to finally broach the subject with my doctor. With tears streaming down my face and barely taking in air, I tried to relay the conversation first to my husband and then to a friend. Crying hysterically the entire time, I explained that the doctor recommended that I go through a few procedures, including surgery, to increase my chances of getting pregnant. It was a step I didn't want to take but at that point I was desperate. Reluctantly, I made an appointment for two weeks later to have the first procedure.

Those two weeks seemed like an eternity. I followed orders to take the cursory laboratory tests and went to sleep extra early the night before because anxiety was getting the best of me. I just wanted to get it out of the way. I awoke the morning of this first procedure feeling just a bit strange. I kept trying to figure out if my period was late. "Maybe I'm just stressed," I thought. I took a pregnancy test because, well, it seemed like the right thing to do. Imagine my surprise, shock and excitement when I realized it was

POSITIVE. I immediately called the doctor's office. His assistant said, *"Oh, we got your lab results. We already knew; we were just waiting for you to come in so we could share the good news with you."*

Imagine that! The entire time that I was boo-hoo crying after my first doctor's visit, God had already worked it out. My son was already forming in my womb. There are so many layers to this story that I don't have the space to tell them all. However, here are a few lessons I learned from this experience:

1. God specializes in the impossible, the difficult and the extraordinary circumstances.
2. God forgives. We are busy punishing ourselves when God has already forgiven us.
3. God operates in a timeframe that is unknown to man.
4. God can show up even in the midst of our doubt.

As women, we unnecessarily beat ourselves up over past mistakes. Don't get me wrong, I wholeheartedly believe that there are consequences for our disobedience; however, we don't get to choose God's reaction to our action. He has forgiven you, moved on and is waiting to shock you with what He has coming in your future. With you, it may not be pregnancy. It may be a new career, a husband, financial prosperity, an illness or a loved one in turmoil. Insert your situation here _____. Know that God specializes in whatever that specific situation is in your life. He is not playing tit for tat with your life. At one time that was hard for me to believe. Yet, my son, Amari Kingston Russell, is living proof of His love, His mercy, and His forgiveness.

Dear Daddy,
Thank You for giving me the desires of my heart. Thank You for loving me so much that You are willing to forgive every single one of my sins – including disobedience. You have blessed me even when my faith isn't whole. I am glad that You are not like man. You don't keep score; instead You cover me in grace and mercy. As I continue to grow in You, help me to be obedient to Your word. Lord, help me also to trust and never doubt You. In Jesus' Name, Amen!

Women of God, today I EMPOWER you to forgive yourself. Seek forgiveness from God and never doubt that He has forgiven you. Move forward with your complete trust in Him, believing that He will do exactly what you ask on His terms and in His timing.

22 WHAT ARE YOU AFRAID OF?
LaKeisha Stringfellow

For God has not given us a spirit of fear and timidity, but of power, love and of self-discipline. 2 Timothy 1:7

When I looked up fear in *Merriam-Webster's Student Dictionary*, here's what I found: *an unpleasant, often strong emotion caused by expectation or awareness of danger. An instance of fear or a state marked by fear. Concern about what may happen. Worry, Dread, Alarm, Fright.*

Hey girlfriend! Did you know that God never intended for fear to cripple you? It's an emotion that we were blessed with, to caution us from danger. But somehow fear began crippling us from reaching our destiny. Someone once told me that, "Our life experiences caused most of our fears." That made me think, and start asking myself, "who told you to be afraid, anyway?" Fear causes so many other things to manifest in your life. Have you ever wondered where stress, depression, anger, frustration, confusion, to name a few, comes from? Fear. When you open the door to fear, you open the door to so many other emotions.

When I thought about being afraid as a child, there is one story that stuck out in my mind. As a kid, and even into some of my adult life, I was terrified of thunderstorms. I remember when it would storm, my grandmother made everyone in the house go into the living room. We had to turn off all lights, televisions and anything else that gave off energy and we just sat in silence, until the storm passed. And honey, you better not answer that telephone! Lightening was going to come through the line and strike you down! My Nana didn't play when it came to those storms.

Now, to Nana's defense, I am sure that she was only imitating how she had been raised. I don't believe at all that she was intentionally planting a seed of fear in us, but she was. As I got older, if it started to even get cloudy outside, the fear would become overwhelming. I would not even be able to sleep peacefully if it was storming. I was always afraid that the lightening was going to for sure kill me dead. I bet you can stop and think of a few childhood memories that will have you laughing, but never even realized that things were being deposited into your spirit man, whether they were positive or negative deposits. Maybe you should take a moment and think back. I can wait. No really, stop for a second and think.

I have lived most of my adult life in fear: fear of success; fear of failure; fear of dying; fear of rejection; fear of storms. I could go on and on, but I am certain you get the picture. I was literally almost afraid of everything until about 5 years ago when I set out on a quest to truly figure out when I became so afraid. For the most part, I had always been adventurous and outgoing. I wasn't sure about what I wanted to do in life, but I wasn't afraid to try new things and step out on faith. It was about 2 years ago, that I started a journey of healing and God uncovered many things about me that had been buried because of fear. I could write an entire book on the basics of fear alone. However, that's not the purpose of this EmpowerMoment. My purpose here is to tell you that you must no longer live in fear. I am here to give you a few pointers on living a life of freedom and prosperity.

Let's go over a few ways for you to overcome fear:

1. **Stop, take a few deep breaths, and think about why you are afraid.**
    - I was scared that I wasn't good enough.
    - I thought, "*Who would even listen to me?*"
    - I didn't think I was smart enough.
    - I didn't know my worth.
2. **When fear begins to rise, don't ignore it.**
    - Ask yourself if you are truly afraid or if you are just nervous. There is a stark difference.
    - Identify the fear in the moment. Determine what's causing you to be afraid.
3. **Walk through the fear.**
    - If you stop, you are only prolonging the process. Stopping allows procrastination to become your friend.
    - Stopping also prolongs the emotion and the fear will then begin to cripple you.
    - If you walk through the fear, you will find courage somewhere in the middle.
    - You become empowered and accomplish goals with more ease.

I hope that in some way, this short passage can help you identify some of your fears. I pray that you are empowered to face them and walk through them to obtain freedom in your life. Your purpose is on the other side of fear. So, you must keep walking and facing daily challenges that empower you to become all that God has called for you to be. Allow fear to serve as a guide to you and not cripple you. You got this! The word of the Lord in **3 John 1:2** says **"Beloved, I wish above all things that thou may prosper and be in health, even as thy soul prospereth."** That sounds like a life free of fear to me!

Dear Daddy,

I ask right now in the name of Jesus that You would cover my mind. Lord God, I want to be free from fear and live the life of power and prosperity that You have promised and purposed for me. Help me to confront my fears and walk in confidence and Holy boldness. Lord, my life belongs to You and today I acknowledge that I am in You. Thank You, Father, for allowing me to recognize fear and move past it. In Jesus' Name, Amen!

Woman of GOD, I EMPOWER you to be free from the fear and bondage of your past. I EMPOWER you to stare fear in the face and run towards it because you have power over fear. I EMPOWER you to talk about your fears because they no longer have power over your choices and thinking. Today, you are free. Today, you are healed. Today, you are walking and living the life of success and freedom that you desire.

23 YOU HAVE SOMETHING TO LIVE FOR!
Kristen R. Harris

"I shall not die, but live, and declare the works and recount the illustrious acts of the Lord." Psalm 118:17 AMP

What happens when all hope is gone and you feel as though you have nowhere to turn? What do you do when it seems as if there is nothing left worth living for? What do you say to the enemy as he torments you with thoughts of suicide? What happens when you don't have the answers to these questions? In efforts to save you from the pit of destruction and death that the enemy wants you to fall into, please let me share my story with you.

Many moons ago, when I was just in elementary school, I contemplated suicide. My family had just moved into a new neighborhood and I was forced to enroll into a new school. I was picked on daily and couldn't seem to rally any allies. Every day I went home feeling defeated and like there was nothing worth living for. In my 6th grade mind, my world was dim and hopeless. That was until one day I met a special instructor at the school. She took me under her wings and reminded me that I was gifted and talented. She showed me just how intelligent I was and used that to catapult me into endeavors that I never imagined I would be a part of. She showed me that I indeed had something to live for.

After I entered high school, my family life took a drastic downturn. Our finances were extremely limited, our home was broken and my mother and I had a very tumultuous relationship. My mother's addiction made her act in ways that assured me that she really didn't love me. And surely if my mother didn't love me, there was nothing worth living for. Thus, I began to re-think my suicidal plans, only that time I was gutsy enough to attempt to carry them out. I tried to slit my wrist to no avail. I took a bottle of pills and waited and waited and waited, but nothing happened. That's when Jesus whispered gently in my ear. *"Daughter, I won't let you die. You have too much at stake. What we have planned for you is going to blow your mind. You have too much to live for; I can't let you go out like this."* That was over 20 years ago and I never once thought about intentionally taking my life again until sometime in 2012.

There I was enjoying life to the fullest, excited about what God was doing and about to do in my life. Everything came to a screeching halt when my walls started to crumble. It seemed as if everything in my life was out of sync. I hated my job, there was chaos in my home, I had no money, I was detached from ministry, I was losing friends, I was an emotional wreck and nothing seemed to be going in my favor. And to top it all off, I was dealing with the pressures, emotions and fears of being pregnant for a third time! With all of this and more happening at one time, I really couldn't focus on one thing worth living for. As I drove into work one morning, I cried as I thought about how I was going to make my final exit. First, I would just run away so that I would have time to really think out my plan. Since my last attempts were unsuccessful, I knew I had to really come with it. No need to be graphic, but let's just say that it was going to indeed be the end that time. By the time I made it to work, my face and neck was stained with salty tear prints. I fixed my face and gained my composure. Once I made it to my desk, I flipped through a home-made calendar that my oldest daughter gave me for Christmas. I was trying to schedule my exit date. As I flipped to June, there were my baby's footprints in the sand. I heard Him whisper gently in my ear, "THAT is what you have to live for."

Ladies, I know that at times life can leave you feeling hopeless and despaired, but know that God created you for a purpose and you too have SOMETHING to live for. Please don't allow the enemy to dupe you into thinking that it won't or can't get better. I promise if you just hold on, stand strong and allow God to be God, your situation will change. And if He doesn't see fit to change the situation, He will change you and the way that you think about what's going on around you. God has you reading this because He interested in seeing you live! He's not going to let you go out like that!

Dear Daddy,
Please forgive me for any time that I contemplated taking the life that You so graciously blessed me with. I understand that it belongs to You and You are just letting me borrow it for an appointed time. Please help me to deal with blows that You allow to come my way. May they never break me, but only strengthen me. Please shut my ear to the enemy when he seeks to tell me that it's over and I may as well give up. I stand on Your words. I render his suicidal attacks harmless and unable to manifest in my life. I declare that I shall live and not die! In Jesus' Name, Amen!

Ladies, today I EMPOWER you to realize that you have so much to live for and LIVE! Meditate on the answers to those questions that you ask yourself when those ugly thoughts of suicide creep into your head:

- What happens when all hope is gone and you feel as though you have nowhere to turn? **The Lord is my Rock, my Fortress, and my Deliverer; my God is my Rock in whom I take refuge. He is my Shield and the Horn my Salvation, my Stronghold! Psalm 18:2 NIV**
  For I the Lord thy God, will hold thy right hand, saying to thee, "Fear not; I will help thee." Isaiah 41:13 KJV

- What do you when it seems as if there is nothing left worth living for? **For we are God's masterpiece. He has created us anew in Christ Jesus, so we can do the good things he planned for us long ago. Ephesians 2:10 NLT**

- What do you say to the enemy as he torments you with thoughts of suicide? **I will not die, but LIVE, and proclaim what the Lord has done. Psalm 118:17 NIV**

- What happens when you don't have the answers to these questions? **If any of you lacks wisdom, he should ask God, who gives generously to all without finding fault, and it will be given to him. James 1:5 NIV**

I Am Growing Better Daily!

"It really takes courage to grow up and become who you really are.

~E. E. Cummings

24 PAIN, PURPOSE & POWER
Lauran A. Smith

Trust in the Lord with all thine heart, and lean not unto thine own understanding. In all thy ways acknowledge him, and he shall direct thy paths. Proverbs 3:5-6 KJV

THE PAIN

It sucks to *feel* like you have wasted 13 years of your life, living in someone else's vision of what reality is supposed to look like. It also sucks not knowing what your ultimate purpose is, while it seems like everyone around you has found theirs.

My story of purpose really began three years and three months after my mother passed away in January 2009. Everything good comes in *threes*, right? Wrong. Not those particular *threes*. I remember feeling like I wasn't who I was supposed to be yet, and that I needed to figure out how to get there. Yet, I didn't feel like I could make it to that point without her. Most days, I was silently angry with God for taking her. The one person who knew me best and supported me the most was gone. Why her though? Those three years after her death, leading up to my purpose, were the hardest years of my life and I questioned God the entire time. I kept my game face on because I had no desire to let anyone close to me know what I was going through, even the ones who were in place and ready to help.

The way that I knew that my purpose was closing in on me was because I couldn't shake the feeling that I was incomplete. My routine was going to a job daily because I saw my parents do the same thing. The only difference between my parents and I was that they were working in the areas that they *wanted* to work in. However, I was absolutely miserable. There were days that I would wake up crying because I had to go to that place. I would even cry on the way to work. My favorite cup of coffee wasn't even able to cheer me up because I still had to go to a job that I absolutely hated. The summer before I graduated from Southern Illinois University (Carbondale), I had an intern with this company, and after graduation, they hired me. I thought it was the right thing to do, so for 13 years, I did the "right thing." And of those 13 years, I was miserable for 12 of them.

Nothing was going to change until I was uncomfortable enough to do something about it. And so it began…

THE PURPOSE

I received mail from the government, advising that I had to do what we all dread--jury duty. But guess what? I was excited to report for duty because that meant that I didn't have to go to work. Yes, it's somewhat sad, but totally true. Now, what I didn't want was to get called for an actual trial, but all I could think of was the fact that I was not going to have to go to work. Once the date rolled around in March of 2012, I woke up *that* particular morning with a smile on my face.

As I sat in the Juror's Room, I pulled out my iPad and a small notebook that I had purchased a few weeks prior. Initially, I started writing letters to various people. I never had plans on actually *sending* them; I just wrote my true feelings in those letters. After those were written, I then started thinking about myself. Who was I really? What did I want out of my life? Was I going to continue to waste away in a high paying, yet highly stressful job? What did my mother see in me that I couldn't see in myself?

The months prior to jury duty, I had taken a liking to all things social media. I started really digging into the social sites, and even found some of my childhood friends from my hometown of Memphis. I then decided that I wanted to do something in the field of creating content. But what would that look like?

After praying about it, and thinking about where my gifts would fit, I came to the decision that I would manage social media sites for those who were otherwise too busy to really post for themselves! I logged into my iPad and came across a celebrity fashion designer and noticed that she didn't really have a strong social media presence. I knew of her events and happenings, but I felt like more people needed to know as well. I thought to myself, "*She needs someone like me.*" In that very moment, I decided on a business name and a tag line. After that, I created all of the content for my website. I also purchased my domain, secured my email addresses and social media channels. I did all of that while sitting in that Juror's Room for eight hours. God spared me that day because I did not get called for a trial. He allowed me the time and space to build my purpose, uninterrupted! The following week, my website was up and running, logo was created, and business cards were on the way! By the time October 2012 came, I had secured my first client--a salon stylist!

I quit the job in April of 2013 and contacted that designer that I mentioned earlier. The very next day after leaving that job, I was hired as her Social Media Manager. I still had my first client and brighter days were certainly ahead of me. I was later given the opportunity to work in the Chicago Public School system as an Assistant Guidance Counselor. However, while working with children, I never gave up on my business and God never gave up on me. As a result, I amassed over 20+ clients, running my business **solo**.

THE POWER

I started waking up every day, smiling and excited about seeing my students! And each evening, I would return home excited to work on my business. I was writing articles for some of the world's most popular bloggers, publications and brands, and I was solicited to become the Publicist Contact for an event that brought super model Beverly Johnson to Chicago. Working with the celebrity fashion designer put me in front of major players in the Chicago business world and I continued to receive opportunity after opportunity. Everything aligned with my purpose. In February 2016, I created Chicago's first ever Black Restaurant Week, and I started this event right on social media, where it all began for me in the first place!

My purpose and power may not have been revealed without the pain of losing my mother. As hurtful as that process was, it truly helped to pull out what God had placed inside of me—the very thing that my mother could see all along! May your purpose be revealed through your pain by praying a similar prayer to the one I did:

Dear Daddy,
You have brought me through the pain of _____. You have given me a new found reason to utilize those things that You have put on the inside of me. Please show me how to use my gifts and passions in the world. Please continue to stand up inside of me, moving me out of the way so that I will not lean unto my own understanding. In Jesus' Name, Amen!

Ladies, today I EMPOWER you to always go with God. Trust Him to use your point of pain as a push to bring forth your purpose and power!

25 BE GRREAT!
Dené M. Brown

Direct my footsteps according to your word... Psalm 119:133 NIV

For about a month, I was facing a tremendous amount of internal battles of worthlessness, self-doubt and perception issues. Most days I laid my head down feeling defeated and insignificant. My good just didn't seem to be good enough. During that time, I reverted to my one of my favorites, the book of Esther, and created this guide.

G-ive into God Not into Stress
Esther didn't put a lot of weight on things out of her control. One sentence in the entire book was given to the trauma of losing her parents. **"Mordecai had taken her as his own daughter when her father and mother died." (Esther 2:7 NIV)** Period...that's it! God is a God that no matter what traumatic experience we face, He will make it a sentence of our story so don't give anything too much. Instead, give it to God.

R-espect the Process, because the Process Respects You
Greatness is a word that seems to follow me. I've had many people use it in conjunction with my purpose and God's plan in my life but I found myself wondering exactly when greatness would hit my life. Oh, it hit me alright. One day I realized greatness doesn't hit, it happens! Greatness is a process. Greatness is waking up at 5am to work out because that's the only time you can or working late on a project instead of pushing it off until tomorrow. Greatness is when you are dead tired from giving the world your all to stay up an extra hour to give God your everything. **"Before a young woman's turn came to go in to King Xerxes, she had to complete twelve months of beauty treatments prescribed for the women, six months with oil of myrrh and six with perfumes and cosmetics." (Esther 2:12 NIV)** Esther was in that process of greatness for 2 years which is 24 months or 730 days! Whew! That's a long time, right?! Actually, it was one verse in her book. One!

R-espect the Process, because the Process Respects You (The Remix)
It seems we get stuck here because for some reason as humans we struggle with control. Respect the process! Say it with me, "Respect, the process!" You have no idea who God is moving out of the way so you can sit on your throne. In Chapter 1, Queen Vashti was killed for "disrespecting" the king (a.k.a. standing her ground), but she was removed so Esther could be queen. God isn't going to allow you to be a mistress in a profession,

relationship or anything else. Your throne is your throne and you won't have to share it with anyone, but you must be patient. Respect your process!

E-ventually It Gets Better
Chapter 9 is entitled "The Triumph of the Jews" and is the longest chapter in the book of Esther. Funny how your preparation may seem like the longest chapter in your book, but just wait because God will make your win even longer! Your victory is greater than anything you've ever been through.

A-re you a Jones? Stop trying to keep up with them. Be you!
Another thing I love about Esther is how she went through. When faced with adversity she didn't pull a Job and rip her clothes off or lament like David. She said, **"Go and get all the Jews living in Susa together. Fast for me. Don't eat or drink for three days, either day or night. I and my maids will fast with you. If you will do this, I'll go to the king, even though it's forbidden. If I die, I die." (Esther 4:16 NIV)** In my spiritual life, I've struggled with identity issues. I don't express my love by shouting loudly all the time. Thus, I struggled with how people perceived me. Esther's process touched me because it wasn't like the people written before her; she did what she felt on her heart to do.

T-reasure Your True Purpose
At the end of reading Esther I reverted to my favorite scripture. **"Rejoice always, pray continually, give thanks in all circumstances; for this is God's will for you in Christ Jesus." (1 Thessalonians 5:16-18 NIV)** I stopped praying for things and just began praying for wisdom. I prayed for wisdom to deal with my day to day, my riches and rags and my friends and foes. I stopped putting weight on life because I'm not driving this car; God is. He continuously shows us that He is God, yet we forget – complicating something that was supposed to be so simple.

Dear Daddy,
I give my life over to You so I can live in peace and freedom. I lean not unto my own understanding, but unto Yours. This is my declaration of love to You that I will not question You, have anxiety over things I can't change or over analyze details like I can do something about them. You are God and at this moment I'm done playing God in my life by trying to figure everything out. I trust You because You sit on the throne in my life. In Jesus' Name, Amen!

Ladies, I EMPOWER you to live! Be a warrior and not a worrier. God's got this! That is a simple sentence but implement it in your life. To live an uncomplicated life just be G.R.R.E.A.T. I EMPOWER

you to, "Rejoice ALWAYS, pray CONTINUALLY and give thanks in ALL circumstances."

26 SIZE DOESN'T EQUATE STRENGTH... MINDSET DOES
Luronda T. Jennings

Don't copy the behavior and customs of this world, but let God transform you into a new person by changing the way you think. Then you will learn to know God's will for you, which is good and pleasing and perfect. Romans 12:2 NLT

Have you ever thought about how life would be if you could completely block out all rules and expectations set by the world? How each day would be if you were the perfect girl? I used to wonder that exact thing until God revealed my purpose and the power of my thinking. You see, the insecurities all started for me when I was in the sixth grade. Kind of early for a young girl, but my strength had not yet been displayed. I walked into gym class and noticed there was a scale sitting against the wall. I hadn't noticed it before but I got really scared when I heard my name being called. *Luronda Jennings, it is your turn to weigh in.* My knees started shaking and my heart trembling within. I didn't notice a difference in me until that day in class. My number was much larger than the other kids I asked. My weight was 199 pounds in the sixth grade. From that day forward I knew that memory would not fade.

I lived a very blessed childhood as an overweight girl. I was never bullied and my parents gave me the world. They kept my brother and me in the nicest clothes and latest shoes. Even if my school or recreational softball team didn't have shorts to fit me, my mother made sure I was not different without making it public news. From my family, friends, and classmates, I never felt ridiculed.

As I journeyed through life, my weight gain continued. Yet, even in my relationships it never was an issue. Years and years went by, and the number on the scale increased and started to burn. My weight fluctuated, my knees ached, and my blood pressure became a concern. High blood pressure and diabetes run in my family. Knowing this, I lost 60 pounds but I gained back 120. I knew it was time to make a permanent change and it wasn't going to be easy. You see, I couldn't button up my size 30/32 pants anymore. So I stood in the mirror dreading the fact that I would have to order clothes out of a magazine and not shop in a store. How and when did that happen and why didn't someone stop me? At that point my actions weren't enough. My mindset needed strengthening.

I prayed and cried, *"Lord please help me."* I asked, *"Why can't I remain healthy?"* I broke down and had a tough conversation with one of my best friends. He committed to helping me until the very end. That day I knew I had to face the same fear I was forced to face as a sixth grader in gym class. I stepped on the scale and let out a huge gasp. 399.6 pounds was the number on the screen. I began to cry but at the same time I was encouraged by the strength my mindset would bring. I had lost weight before so I knew my strength wasn't in my size. Now that my mindset was more determined, I couldn't believe my eyes. This time I wasn't so concerned about becoming physically small. I was more concerned about permanently strengthening my mindset once and for all.

There are four actions that God allowed me to realize that helped to strengthen my mindset and transform my life. It doesn't matter if you are trying to become a healthier woman, start a business, or finish school, these 4 actions will guarantee a stronger mindset.

- Setting small goals - Set small goals that lead up to the bigger goal. This action increases focus, perseverance, and self-confidence. For example, setting a small goal of losing 10 pounds each month is very realistic and you'll look up in 5 months and see a healthier woman.
- Documenting progress - Whether you are journaling every day, taking pictures of yourself, or keeping track of your caloric intake, documenting your progress is very important. It helps with boosting your self-esteem and keeping you emotionally stable. Seeing personal progress makes it difficult to give up.
- Keeping encouraging scriptures/quotes nearby - Placing encouraging scriptures/quotes on your mirror, in your car, on your desk at work, and on the refrigerator, help keep you motivated throughout the whole day. We all need motivation.
- Celebrating success - Ladies, you deserve celebration. I'm not talking about throwing yourself a party every time you lose a pound or pay off a bill yet embracing small activities that you enjoy. It could be as small as buying yourself a new shade of lipstick or fingernail polish to getting a massage or trying a new hair color. Just to something that makes you feel even more awesome.

Within one year and a half I lost 110 pounds, got down to a size 18/20, and I feel great. Yes, I am working on losing more weight but I am no longer concerned with the size that I'm expected to be in order to be considered a perfect girl in the eyes of the world. I am more concerned with having a stronger mindset that will allow me to be a perfect girl in the eyes of the Lord. When your mindset is tight, and your actions are right, then your growth will take flight. A strong mindset will empower *every* area of your life.

Dear Daddy,
When I look in the mirror I may not always see the woman You created me to be. At times I may feel insecure about my size and I become focused on becoming physically smaller. Although, I realize becoming physically smaller may be good for my health, I ask that You help me strengthen my mindset. I may not feel strong in my current body but I ask that You help me strengthen my mindset so that I may be a stronger woman in You. In Jesus Name, Amen!

Ladies, today I EMPOWER you to find your strength in your mindset. Use your thoughts to help guide your actions, in order for you to grow into the woman God created you to be. I EMPOWER you to be intentional about the information you absorb because your mindset has the ability to EMPOWER everything.

27 FOCUS ON YOUR STRENGTHS, MANAGE YOUR WEAKNESSES
Tchicaya Ellis Robertson

Cast not away therefore your confidence, which hath great recompense of reward. For ye have need of patience, that, after ye have done the will of God, ye might receive the promise. Hebrews 10:35-36 KJV

As I was sitting in my Leading Extraordinary Teams training the other day, I was humbled to see that one of the findings in the research behind the training module is that, *"The highest levels of performance come when we are focusing on strengths, while managing weaknesses."* This message resonated with me because it is also one of the key principles discovered in the research behind my first book, *Motivated by Passion, Held Back by Fear.* That same principle in different words is, "Develop your natural talent."

God has given us all a talent to share with the world. The scripture implies that if we are confident in what He has given us we will receive the rewards that He has already set aside for us. As long as we're doing the will of God, we will reach our goals.

Let me break it down for you! Stop focusing on what you can't do, what you don't have, what you don't like, who you don't like, who didn't do this for you, and who didn't do that for you. Forget all of that and start thinking about what you can do, what you do have, what you do like, who compliments you and who helps you. Focus on that and watch how your perspective changes. Being positive is so much more fun, right? Think about that Sally Sad Face that brings the whole place down when she enters a room. Do you want to be that girl?

I want you to stop and think about all the things that make you, you! What are all the things that make you your best you? What are all the things that make you your worst you? Take out a piece of paper (or your phone) and jot down three things that you do exceptionally well. Are you the best cook ever? Are you a great writer? Do people come to you for advice because you're a great listener? What do you do well? These are your strengths. These are your God-given talents. These are the things that you do naturally well or at least enjoy doing.

Now, about that list of things that make you your worst you. Toss them. Throw them out! Burn them! Delete them out of your consciousness – and your mobile device. Forget about them. Because your challenge for today is to remember how totally awesome you are! Who is the greater you? Who is the best you? What strengths will you show the world today?

How will you channel that strength to achieve your goals? What are you trying to do? Start a business? Change careers? Finish college? End a relationship? Get a promotion at your job? How will you use your strength to get what you want? How will you channel what you do best, to get what you want?

Dear Daddy,
Please help me channel my energy into using my strengths to accomplish what You created me to do. May I use every gift, every skill, every talent and every strength to grow into everything that I am destined to be. In Jesus' Name, Amen!

Ladies, today I EMPOWER you to look in the mirror. I EMPOWER you to list the three things that you do exceptionally well. Read them to yourself. Convince yourself, again, that these things are good enough. Say to yourself, "I am worthy. I am strong. My weaknesses don't define me. But my strengths do."

28 CAN YOU REALLY HANDLE IT?
Yerinita T. Curtis-Fuller

Come to me, all you who are weary and burdened, and I will give you rest. Take my yoke upon you and learn of me, for I am gentle and humble in heart, and you will find rest for your souls. For my yoke is easy and my burden is light. Matthew 10:28-30 NIV

God gave us the gift of life; it is up to us to give ourselves the gift of living well. -Voltaire

"*I got this!*" "*No, I can handle it.*" "*No thank you; I don't need anyone's help.*" Sound familiar? Those statements eventually become: "*I'm tired and overwhelmed.*" "*I can't do this anymore! I quit!*" Why? Because we were not created to carry anything alone. Perhaps you were raised in an "I can handle everything by myself" environment. I can speak from personal experience that this kind of mentality is a recipe for disaster. I had this mindset. I learned to reject the help that God had sent me. In doing so, I was rejecting God. This kind of mentality contributed to an emotional, physical, mental and spiritual breakdown. I intentionally and unintentionally took on entirely too much. I begin to experience burn out and eventually, I began lacking the motivation to perform what was necessary for a healthy everyday life. I wondered, "How did I get to such a low place?" The truth is I didn't accept the help.

God did not create you and me without the necessity of needing help. He gave Eve to Adam and called her his helper. A strong-willed woman, whether single or married, sometimes struggles to bring balance to what has always been demanded of her. Independence can be the gift and the curse. I was raised by a single mom. Witnessing my mother handle everything alone indirectly taught me to do the same. Asking for help was seen as a sign of weakness. I didn't understand that asking for help was actually a sign of strength.

It's not easy admitting that you cannot do it alone or that you don't have it all together. It was never meant for me to carry this alone. Girlfriend, it's not meant for you to carry it alone either. There are definitely consequences to not balancing what we can do alone versus what we need help to carry. We were created to need support. When I handled it on my own for too long weariness took over my daily functionality. What once seemed easy for me then became like heavy yokes around my neck. What I thought I was handling started handling me. The weariness from the burdens got so heavy that the only choice left was to die in it or cry out for help. The lack of acknowledging and accepting that I needed help would have eventually killed me. I experienced anxiety attacks, weight gain, fear, high blood pressure and loss of relationships just to name a few. I was tired, overwhelmed, stressed and worried beyond normality. Some of these "burdens" even led to prescription medicine.

My rest finally came in the taking. Taking His yoke upon me which was easy. My rest came in going to Jesus and confessing that I needed Him. For His yoke is easy and His burden light. Jesus wanted to help me carry this all along. He desired that I walk in His rest, even with the many roles He had entrusted me with. Sis, resting equals trusting. I had to trust that Jesus would help me carry these burdens if I was willing to let go of the controls. I entered His rest by realizing that He loves me so much and that He would do anything for me. I learned that anything I entrusted to Him would be in good hands. I learned to let Him help me to "handle it."

I rested in trusting Him to daily provide for my family. (**Philippians 4:19**)
I rested in trusting Him to heal my husband and children. (**Exodus 15:26**)
I rested in trusting Him to provide a home for us after three years of wandering. (**Zechariah 3:16**)
I rested by trusting Him to restore relationships that He had ordained in my life. (**Deuteronomy 30:3-13**)
I rested by allowing Him to deliver me from fear of my future. (**Jeremiah 29:11**)

Will you also trust for your help that comes through trusting in Him? Are you ready to be released from the burden of handling it all alone?

1. Acknowledge: You must come out of denial. You cannot handle it alone. You need the Lord's help and the help of others. Learn to ask for the help and receive the help so things are lighter for you.
2. Prioritize: Share the load with others. Also, remove things that God reveals shouldn't be on your plate. This step will take discipline and courage.
3. Maintain: Take inventory often. Are the responsibilities being shared? Make sure you are not piling things back on your plate. Remember Jesus makes it easier, lighter and better.

Dear Daddy,
I realize that I have tried to do this on my own and failed. I acknowledge right now that I need Your help. I want to walk in Your rest by trusting You to help me to carry my burdens. Today, I let go of being independent of You. Today, I partner with You and receive Your yoke which is easy and Your burden which is light. In Jesus' Name, Amen!

Women Who Are Burned Out, I EMPOWER you to recognize that you cannot do life alone. Jesus is here to help you with every single

burden. He is always waiting and willing to make things easier for you. Call on Him and He will answer you.

29 PROJECT: TAMING MY TONGUE
LaVonna V. Fields

With the tongue we praise our Lord and Father, and with it we curse human beings, who have been made in God's likeness. Out of the same mouth come praise and cursing. My brothers and sisters, this should not be. James 3:9-10 NIV

Growing up, I would sing the following words in church: *"Let the words of my mouth and the mediation of my heart, be acceptable in thy sight."* These words would be sung right before the Lord's Prayer. I never thought about the words until I began studying the book of James, chapter 3. I can recall how frustrated I was because I knew that I had to tame my tongue and I stopped studying James because I did not want to change.

Up until that point in my life, I believed that "my truth" was something that people should hear and I did not hold my tongue for anyone. I would talk about people to their face and behind their backs. If I did not like a person, I wanted others to not like them as well. Therefore, I would "tell my truth" about the person in question to anyone that would listen, so that they would not be friends with them. That behavior ultimately made me a bully and a manipulator. Then in my next breath, I would shout and sing praises to God.

It's funny how when you have to learn a lesson, that no matter how you avoid it, God has ways to get your attention. I recall going to lunch with a co-worker who I could tell was a Christian by her speech and actions. She asked me if I was okay with her saying a prayer before we ate. I had no problem with that. Her prayer was simple and short; however, her words still affect me 10 years later. She asked the Lord to let our conversation be a blessing to one another, and that our words honor Him and that we leave out the gossip and any words that may be offensive unto Him. I sat there quietly after her prayer and I recalled all of the times that I would try to gossip with her about other staff members in our department; or when I would use offensive words when I was angry or upset. She would always redirect my comments in a nice and gentle way. However, her prayer cut deep into my heart and that time I said, "I hear you Lord! I am ready to change."

I remember going back to the study of James, chapter 3. I realized that even though the tongue is the smallest part of the human body (**James 3:5**) that it has the power to give life or death (**Proverbs 18:21**). I decided at that moment that I wanted my tongue to be a spring of life and that I needed God to help me tame it. I wish I could say that the next day I mastered the control over my tongue but that would be a huge lie.

However, through studying God's Word and prayer, the ongoing project of taming my tongue began.

To begin this journey, I searched the Bible for scripture text that could be stored in my mind and written in my heart (**Hebrews 8:10**) as tools to control my tongue. The Holy Spirit led me to understand that whatever my heart is full of, it will certainly come out of my mouth. (**Matthew 12:34**) If my heart is full of evil, hatred, jealousy, selfishness, and other deceitful things then it will manifest in my conversations. (**Matthew 15:17-19**) Therefore, I had to ask God's forgiveness and for Him to create in me a new heart. (**Psalm 51:10**)

Secondly, I had to focus my energy on being silent (**1 Thessalonians 4:11**), listening to what people have to say and not rush my response. I learned in a public speaking course, that there is value in pausing before I give a response. The pause gives me an opportunity to ask God for the right words to say and for me to control any negative emotions that I may be feeling. I also can determine through this pause if I should say anything at all. Sometimes remaining quiet is the best thing to do.

Finally, be slow to anger. (**Proverbs 15:18**) Always try to choose to have patience and compassion for others. By staying calm, I have been able to give wisdom and instruction in a kind and calming voice. (**Proverbs 31:26**) I am not saying that following these three steps has been easy, but when you allow the Holy Spirit control over your heart, your mouth, and your emotions then *Project: Taming the Tongue* is attainable.

Dear Daddy,
Please forgive me for words of death that I have spoken consciously and subconsciously to those whom I have come into verbal contact with. Help me to tame my tongue by filling my heart with Your love and Your words so that I can speak life to those who are hurting. Help me to be quiet and listen, slow to anger, and consult You before I speak. In Jesus' Name, Amen!

Women of God, I EMPOWER you to tame your tongue by letting go of the negative things in your heart. Allow God to fill your heart with His love. Then you can praise Him with a pure heart and speak life into all of your relationships.

Can't Stop, Won't Stop!

"Never give up, for that is just the place and time that the tide will turn.

~Harriet Beecher Stowe

30 DON'T STOP!
Latasha L. McCrary

"Jesus told his disciples a parable to show them that they should always pray and not give up." Luke 18:1 NIV

Feel like giving up? Prayed so long that you feel like throwing in the towel? Are you exhausted, overwhelmed, or even discouraged from trying? If any of this applies to you, God is saying DON'T STOP TRYING!

As a youth, I was a huge fan of Michael Jordan. At times, I revisit his book *I Can't Accept Not Trying*. In it he writes, "I realized that if I was going to achieve anything in life I had to be aggressive. I had to get out there and go for it. I don't believe you can achieve anything by being passive…That's not to say there aren't obstacles or distractions. If you're trying to achieve, there will be roadblocks…But roadblocks don't have to stop you. If you run into a wall, don't turn around and give up. Figure out how to climb it, go through it, or work around it."

I thought about these words and how they relate to our spiritual walk. How do we respond when we encounter life's roadblocks? Do we become more aggressive or do we simply turn around and give up? In the gospel of Luke, Jesus tells two parables which speak directly to how God desires for us to handle moments when we feel like giving up. In short, Jesus tells us not to give up.

In the first parable, Jesus says suppose you go to a friend's house at midnight to ask for food only to be turned away. He explains that although the friend may not give you what you ask for the first time, **"if you keep knocking long enough, he will get up and give you whatever you need because of your shameless persistence." (Luke 11:8 NLT)** Now, think about this. The fact that you would go to a friend's at midnight means that there is likely a dire need. You're not asking for the fun of it; you're asking because you have a need that you believe your friend can meet. Have you ever asked God for something in your midnight hour? Did you feel as if you weren't getting what you needed when you asked? Well, through this parable Jesus teaches us that *if you are truly in need why stop asking?* Jesus encourages us to **"keep on asking, and you will receive what you ask for. Keep on seeking, and you will find. Keep on knocking, and the door will be opened to you. For everyone who asks, receives. Everyone who seeks, finds. And to everyone who knocks, the door will be opened." (Luke 11:9-10 NLT)**

Similarly, **"Jesus told his disciples a parable to show them that they should always pray and not give up." (Luke 18:1 NIV)** In the parable, there is a widow who goes before an unjust judge in order to receive relief against her adversary. Jesus says that for some time the judge refused the widow, but eventually he gave her justice because she kept bothering him. The parable concludes by reminding us that we should expect more from God than from an unjust judge. **"And will not God bring justice for his chosen ones, who cry out to him day and night? Will he keep putting them off? I tell you, he will see that they get justice, and quickly." (Luke 18:7 NIV)**

This parable demonstrates that if we can go before men and continue to ask for worldly things, we should be even bolder when we approach our Father who is just and loves us. Jesus says that *God will answer those who cry out to Him day and night.* So, although you may feel tired, weary, or even dismayed, God does not want you to give up. Keep praying despite how you feel. **"Pray in the Spirit at all times and on every occasion. Stay alert and be persistent in your prayers." (Ephesians 6:18 NLT)** Remember that in due time, God will answer and reward your diligence. **"So let's not get tired of doing what is good. At just the right time we will reap a harvest of blessing if we don't give up." (Galatians 6:9 NLT)**

Dear Daddy,

Thank You for being a God who answers prayer. Teach us how to be persistent and not give up at the first sign of defeat. Remind us that faith requires us to maintain hope even when all visible evidence seems contrary to our belief. Help us to walk by faith and not by sight. Renew us daily and allow Your Holy Spirit to speak encouragement to our hearts. In Jesus' Name, Amen!

Ladies, I EMPOWER you to stay on the course. Don't give up! When you feel like throwing in the towel, continue to pray, knowing that God is a rewarder of those who diligently seek Him.

31 RUN ON IN THE RAIN!
Kristen R. Harris

**Who cut in on you to keep you from obeying the truth?
Galatians 5:7 NIV**

"Brown sugar melts in the rain!" This has been my retort for anyone who has requested that I participate in anything while it's raining out for as long as I can remember. I don't want to go anywhere, see anyone or do anything if it is raining outside. I am just not keen on exploring the world on rainy days; I'd rather stay inside, safe from all of the elements! So imagine my disgust one evening as I was out for a jog around my neighborhood and the sky opened to water the earth.

About 30 minutes into my run, I noticed the clouds beginning to gather and the sky turning dark. Thus, I picked up my pace because I was determined to make it home before it began to rain. Moments later I felt the first small drop on my cheek. I needed to get home before the real downpour came so I sped up a bit more. But I didn't make it. Torrential-like rain pounded on the pavement as I struggled to see my way home. In that moment, I contemplated making four different choices: (1) just stopping under a tree for shelter and letting the rain pass (2) slowing down to a nice brisk walk instead of jogging (3) calling my husband to come and pick me up (4) pressing through the rain and completing my run. I must be honest and say that choice number 1 was the most reasonable and pleasing one to me, and I was looking for a nice, friendly tree to hide under. However, as I searched for shelter, I couldn't find one good tree. That's when God spoke to me. He said, *"You were running a good race. Who cut in on you to keep you from obeying the truth? A little rain? Are you going to let a little rain hinder your plans? Is an unexpected downpour going to throw you off course from going where you intended to go and doing what you dreamed of accomplishing?"*

As tough as that was to swallow and as much as I was not feeling it, I maintained my speed and kept jogging. Did it feel good? Absolutely not! I could barely see as the water clouded my vision and my soggy hair began to fall into my face. My wet clothes were adding extra weight to my run. I was truly exhausted! But I didn't stop; I kept running. I even cried a bit because the burn in my legs seemed to intensify. But I didn't stop; I kept running.

What seemed like an eternity later (but was really only about a minute later), I reached a completely dry spot. I looked up expecting to see a gathering of trees holding back the rain but there was only an unobstructed view to the sky. It was not raining there and from the looks of the ground, it had never been raining in that spot. However, I turned around and it was still raining behind me! That's when I got the revelation. I made a choice to push through my storm and once I did, God brought me to a sunny, dry place! I didn't wait for the storm to pass; I pushed past my storm!

Sisters, there are going to be many rainy seasons in your life. But you must run on. You cannot allow any circumstances to cut in on you and stop your progress. Often times, God just wants to see if you are willing to continue running the race in the midst of the storm to reveal if you are really as faithful as you claim you are. It's like He is asking, *"Do you really want what you asked for? If so, why are you stopping? Do you really trust Me like you say that you do? If so, then why don't you believe that I am right here running in the rain with you?"* When you change your mind and decide to push through regardless of the circumstances, you will be pleasantly surprised at how quickly you will be out of the storm. Just like me, you may find it very difficult to see as you run in the rain. But run anyway! If you are willing to press on, He will lead you when you cannot see your way out of the storm!

Knowing how much I absolutely detest being in the rain, and still completed my run gave me a new sense of accomplishment. It gave me the confidence to believe that I can truly overcome challenges. Your rainy patch is for your development. Do not stunt your growth because you would rather hide under a tree while the storm passes. Or even worse, phone a friend who you think can save you from the storm. Run on in the rain! After all, the rainy days are what makes beautiful things grow!

Dear Daddy,
I know that sometimes I do not willingly submit to pushing through the rainy days of my life. Please help me when I try to resist my growth process. I am committed to growing in You, and if that means that I have to experience some storms, then please help me endure. I know that I can rest confident in knowing that even in every downpour, You are my shelter! Thank You for my rainy days because they are helping me to blossom into a beautiful flower! In Jesus' Name, Amen!

Ladies, today I EMPOWER you to simply run in the rain! You may be experiencing a storm in the areas of relationships, finances, losing a loved one or anything else, but know that the One who allows rain to come knows how much you will grow from this storm! I EMPOWER you to not just wait for the storm to pass, but to outrun your storm! Leave the rain behind you!

EPILOGUE

WOW! What a journey this has been! We kicked it off with learning how to really be Superwomen and slay with full tanks! Hopefully, now you are okay with crying being your badge of strength and not your weakness. If you have Mommy and Daddy issues, you should now know that everything can be reconciled through your Daddy in heaven! And here on earth, there is a woman, somewhere that has dealt with what you are currently experiencing. If God brought her out unscathed, He can do it again in your circumstances. After all, God's got you girl!

Now that you are even more confident of His love for you, I pray that you are secure in your love for yourself! You are pretty darn amazing girl! You have been set free and when He sets you free, you are free indeed. With this newfound freedom, continue to grow better every single day. Your growth is not just for you; it is for someone who is waiting for you to become everything that God created you to be so that she too can grow into what God created her to be.

Equipped with everything you need for the journey, don't you ever dare consider stopping or giving up. God did not bring you this far just to bring you this far. You are victorious; you are loved; you are more than a conqueror; you are God's best handiwork! Own it and keep pressing, sister.

This book was never designed to be a one-time read. Now that you have completed the 31-day journey, revisit this as often as you need to be reminded how God brought us out. He is no respecter of persons. Thus, He can perform similar miracles of healing, deliverance, transformation and favor in your life too. Remember, this is not a book for hoarding! We shared our stories to EMPOWER you, so now it's your turn. Be sure to share our stories with women who you know need to hear them. In fact, be sure to share *your* story too!

Until next time, be empowered!

~Kristen R. Harris

MEET TIFFANY T. HUFF

Tiffany T. Huff is a Pittsburgh, Pennsylvania native where she now lives with her husband and two preteen sons. Tiffany is the Founder of The Tiffany Huff Experience, inclusive of Reinventing You Podcast & Tour, The Coffee & Clarity Experience, and Write for Your Life Publishing. Her second book, 30 Day Stay: A Story of Escaping Death, Healing from Heartbreak and Finding Hope in Homelessness later in 2017.

She studied Communications & Professional Writing as an undergraduate at Carlow University and Higher Education Management at the Graduate School of Education at The University of Pittsburgh.

Tiffany believes the ultimate form of self-care is to honor yourself by honoring who God created you to be and doing what He created you to do and encourages women to hustle higher, unto God as opposed to hustling harder according to the world. Her gifts of clarity, insight and passion for challenging women to overcome their fears to reinvent themselves as the women they were called and created to be are the fuel for manifesting God's masterpiece of her life. Tiffany believes strongly in the power of the pen and the necessity of women to share their stories not only to heal themselves, but as an act of service to help other women heal as well.

You can learn more about Tiffany and her work at www.Tiffany-Huff.com.

WHO IS KRISTEN R. HARRIS?

Who is Kristen R. Harris, you ask? Well, I am really just a girl with big dreams who decided to go for it! I have been writing for as long as I can remember and in 2016, I finally decided to turn this passion into a profit. Everything that I do is to fulfill my purpose of empowering women around the globe. I subscribe to the notion that every woman is full of potential and purpose but many lack the knowledge on how to get everything out that is inside of them. My job is to help draw it out by equipping women with the tools that they need to get unstuck. As a figurative midwife I help women realize that they are PREGNANT with purpose and PUSH past their pain to DELIVER everything that God has promised them.

As a wife to an amazing man, mother to three young princesses and a serial entrepreneur, I thoroughly understand the juggling act of running a home and multiple businesses. Thus, on those rare occasions when I can take a breather, you can find me snuggled under a plush blanket with fuzzy socks on as I read a thought provoking book. See, just a simple girl residing in a complex world!

Of course, there is much more that I could share. However, you just finished reading a whole book; you don't want to hear anything about me! But just in case you do, you can find out more about me by visiting my website: www.kristenrharris.com.

For information on all of the contributing authors, please visit www.empowermoments.org.

Made in the USA
Middletown, DE
06 May 2017